THE RITE PLACE

Kids Do Church!
Adults Do Too!

SHAWN M. SCHREINER AND DENNIS E. NORTHWAY

Morehouse Publishing
NEW YORK · HARRISBURG · DENVER

Morehouse Publishing, 4785 Linglestown Road, Suite 101, Harrisburg, PA 17112

Morehouse Publishing, 19 East 34th Street, New York, NY 10016

Morehouse Publishing is an imprint of Church Publishing Incorporated.
www.churchpublishing.org

Cover design: Laurie Westhafer

Interior design and production: Helen H. Harrison; liturgy section: Robin Lybeck

Library of Congress Cataloging-in-Publication Data
(to come)

Printed in the United States of America

ISBN: 978-0-8192-2945-8

*To the staff, children, parents, vestry, and parishioners of
Grace Episcopal Church, Oak Park, Illinois past and present.*

*To my parents, Jean Porter and John Schreiner, and spouse,
Victoria L. Garvey, who have always encouraged me to be
the child of God that I was made to be.*

Shawn

*To all my beautiful and dedicated choir members
at Grace Episcopal Church, Oak Park, past and present;
your lives and voices have given wings
to my faith and my song!*

Soli deo Gloria!

Dennis

Table of Contents

Acknowledgements

MY EARLIEST MEMORIES OF CHURCH ARE OF GREAT TALL people standing in front of me, getting up and down from the pews, flipping through books, chatting, singing, and walking up for that food and drink that was handed out by people in funny looking outfits.

I remember going to confession every day—okay, it seemed like every day—and telling the priest my sins (even though I was not sure what that meant). Mostly I remember Fr. Jim who talked to us like we were real people and would take the time to answer any questions we had and arranged for me to get home when I was sick. Then there were the good people of tiny St. Luke's who did not freak out when five children arrived at their doorstep one Epiphany. Fr. Miles invited my sister and another youth to do a dialogue sermon and set me free to organize a seminar on domestic violence. All of those early Christian formation folks who made the stories come alive and found creative ways for us to have Sunday school during the thirty to forty-five minute sermons.

Who can forget Bishop Ted Jones, Diocese of Indianapolis, who would gather on a monthly basis with the youth council. He had the willingness to open the doors of his diocesan office wide to a very opinionated young person who had demands about youth presence for the Episcopal Diocese of Indianapolis. Hats off to Jack Eastwood, Jackie Means, and All Saints' Indianapolis who were early trendsetters for youth serving on a vestry.

All of this is to say that my formative years were mostly filled with people, churches, and places that valued the presence of children and youth in their worship spaces and in the overall life and ministries of the congregations. For sure there have been some who would have loved to have children seen and not heard. Surely all of these experiences shaped my lay ministry days as well as my ordained years.

We are all the Body of Christ with ministries to offer to the world and to our congregations. That was the overwhelming message that was given to this child of God. It is the central message that I pray we have brought into The Rite Place.

This book has been a gift to write. I am so very thankful for the staff at Grace and their willingness to be a part of the journey of creating The Rite Place and giving feedback in the writing of the book. My spouse, Victoria Garvey, is always my inspiration and cheerleader in the ministries that God has given me—including this book.

Shawn Schreiner

Acknowledgements

THERE IS AN ONGOING NATIONAL PROJECT CALLED "StoryCorps" which gives an interviewer the chance to ask someone very close to them, ultimate questions about their lives. The questions posed are ones similar to, "For what would you like to have your life remembered?" or "What was ultimately most important to you?" They are given forty minutes for the interview and it is then stored in the Library of Congress. Most of them, like final conversations of terminal patients, focus on: "Thank you," "I love you," "I forgive you," or "Forgive me."

When I am quiet, and I spend a lot of time in silence because the production of sound is what I "do," my heart immediately goes to gratitude. I am so grateful for so many things. I was born to do what I do—to give people their song. There is almost no way to express what a deep honor it is to make this my life's work. This is an intimate and deeply spiritual vocation, and takes an immense amount of love and attention to do it well. My hope is that I have done it well. One cannot do this in a vacuum. For this immense gift, I say thank you.

I pray often, and my prayers are always filled with the earnest request for light perpetual to shine on those on the path that have died. These have walked with me and no longer do so. Each of these people have had an important part in forming me to do the work to which I have been born, that eventually led to this book. To Welly Alaway, Elizabeth Candlish, Gary and Susie Zwicky, Sherman Kraus, Michael Smith, David Porkola, Dolores and Wayne Northway, Grace Auer, Fred Larsen, Barb Weith, Shirley Levitan, and Robert C. Van Kooten, please know I love you.

I am a very flawed person and need a community to continue to uphold me and form me. This spiritual community is larger than the parish that I serve; it is the circles-that-intersects-circles of the areas of my life. I would be a poorer soul with the removal of any one. Each component of my life: my students, my singers, my colleagues, my friends, and my family have been on the "team" to teach me how to be me. I have tried my best, but do not always succeed and, for that, to whom I have failed, I am sorry.

I also need to, very quietly, thank God.

A book about worship, a book about forming young people and about giving them their song comes about because many, many separate interactions have taken place in my life that have safely delivered me to The Rite Place.

Dennis Northway A.K.A. denden

Foreword

SOMETHING EXCITING IS HAPPENING AT GRACE CHURCH IN Oak Park, Illinois. It happens every Sunday at 9:00 a.m. In the setting of a large, elaborate, neo-gothic building, a group of children and adults of all ages gathers to do some rather simple things. They greet one another. They sing easily learned songs. They tell and hear the stories of faith. They share signs and symbols of the life we all share. They set a table with simple food, bread and wine, enough for all. They pray. They share the bread and the cup. And in these simple, very human actions, they encounter the presence of the living God, they meet the Risen Jesus. Sometimes in ways that take their breath away. Sometimes in ways that help to change their lives. They do these things and encounter God together. All are involved. Everyone contributes. Everyone receives. Everyone leads. And everyone follows.

This book is an account of a congregation that is taking seriously the implications of the church's conviction that baptism is full inclusion in the Body of Christ. For too long Christians have created and enforced divisions in the church. In spite of our official theology of baptism, in the face of the biblical witness that in the Body of Christ there is no justification for any divisions based on class or gender or race or any of the other categories human beings have invented to divide ourselves. And while we have made some progress in dismantling some of those divisions, the status of children in the Christian community remains too often unaddressed. Kids are still often treated as less than the fully initiated members of the baptized community they are.

For decades the canons of the Episcopal Church and the *Book of Common Prayer* have presumed that the only prerequisite for the reception of Holy Communion is Holy Baptism. Among other things, that means that even the youngest children are appropriate communicants—from the day of their baptism. This has become more and more the actual practice of congregations across the church and has had a profound and unfolding impact on our understanding of the relationship of both sacraments to the Christian life. Infants and very young children have taught us much about the grace of receptivity. The Christian life does not depend on sophisticated intellectual concepts. And while adult disciplines of theological inquiry are God's gift to us too, we must remember that we do not *think* our way into salvation any more than we can work our way there. God's love is pure gift. Jesus could not have been clearer that children, by their example of simple receptivity, show us the way to the Reign of God.

The leaders of Grace Church have taken very deliberate steps to realize the implications of the full inclusion of children. Not just the communion of children from the time of their baptism, but their roles as disciples, as ministers, as leaders and, yes, teachers within the community and according to their own varied gifts. In this book you will read stories about that work. You will hear about successes and failures. You will find examples of a congregation trying above all to be faithful to Jesus who welcomed children into his embrace and who told his adult disciples to follow their example. This is an account of their work. The challenge to all of us is to do our own.

Jeffrey D. Lee, XII Bishop of Chicago

Introduction

A Congregational Path

Episcopalians firmly believe that our praying shapes our believing. We are formed as the people of God in what we pray, in our prayers, music, and actions. The beginning of formation for all of us, including our children, begins in worship. Worship explains what Episcopalians believe, how we describe God, and how we understand scripture more than anything else. The staff and congregation of Grace Episcopal Church in Oak Park, Illinois created a worship service that brings liturgy (the work of the people), alive in very profound ways to adults and children. We call it, "The Rite Place. Kids Do Church! Adults Do Too!"

"The chicken or the egg." That is an age-old question. In the development of The Rite Place, what came first probably really does not matter. It all has been a journey of a congregation paying attention to our story, the biblical story, and the story of the community around us.

Every year we take our youth choirs on tour. The 2005 destination was Washington D.C. and St. Columba's Episcopal Church was the Sunday morning singing spot. At the end of the service Dennis dropped a bulletin with a description of a thirty-minute worship service for families with children five and under into Shawn's hands and said, "I think we should do this." The phrase in the bulletin that stuck out the most was, "When you talk to children about God all listen." Such a profound truth. A seed had been planted for us and soon for others.

Meanwhile, back at Grace, we were struggling financially. We had decided to do a campaign inviting members of the congregation to give a donation of $250. If each household could make that sacrifice we could make it through the summer and the year. Donation after donation came in. One came with a letter: "I will be glad to give you this donation; but, you need to know that I am not sure that our family will be staying at Grace. We do not feel that our children are really wanted in the service." That had a sting and stayed with us. That letter became a foundation for later conversations. Some might say it was the straw that broke the camel's back and took us on the next step of starting The Rite Place.

Formational Worship

It is somewhat difficult to describe just when the plans for The Rite Place service started. In many ways it was a series of events that pushed us to take such a bold step. Funny thing is that when we look at where we are now it is so hard to remember that the road was complicated as well as easy, filled with tension and joy, fun to envision; it brought great strain and resulted in stronger community. The list could go on. The Rite Place was created out of a perceived need to more fully include children (and their families) in a liturgy that spoke to them on their developmental level. We added an additional service to our Sunday schedule. Based on the outline An Order for

Celebrating the Holy Eucharist (*Book of Common Prayer*, p. 400), it is only thirty minutes long. It is child-centered. Music is integral, as is movement and active participation. And it has made a huge difference in the life of our congregation

Nine years have passed since we first had the thoughts to start The Rite Place. We have learned a lot about worship and its place in the life of the assembly and the community, about ourselves as evangelists, worship leaders and visionaries, and about helping people to understand the Episcopal Church and our style of worship and theology.

When we use our hands and voices we often engage our hearts. When we sing in worship, we are together saying, "I believe this." Songs in Christian worship are creedal. We have spent our lives working with children, watching them grow, seeing them change, answering their questions with more questions, and helping them find their own song. Each person has a song. For some it is not fully formed. For others the song is only in seed. Formation — lifelong formation — is about finding and forming, writing and wrestling, hearing and sharing, singing and whispering one's own song.

Adults see through the eyes of children and children help parents to believe and see in new ways. Beware. We have to be very careful what we do or say. The children and adults with whom we interact are learning! They are listening. As we live with children and interact with them, they are watching and learning. What we do actually forms them in faith and in life. Children have an innate sense of when people are not being authentic with them. They are not skeptical, they just know. We need to approach the holy interaction with children, adults, and worship in an authentic and engaging manner. We invite you to this challenge and the possibilities that are there inside these sacred interactions.

It doesn't surprise us at the Eucharist that the little ones who come forward may not be able to articulate that they want to offer that important bread to others. We don't find it odd that a six-month-old grows still with the sound of the bell, or that someone goes to the storyteller chair to get an apron to be one of the communion ministers, or that someone raises a hand to lead us in worship, or an adult asks to sit with the children to set the table. This is our common Sunday life.

One could say that there are many intergenerational services available, so why this one and why us? We offer this book to the wider church because we (with the staff of Grace Church) believe that we have created something that the church needs. Our worship service engages children and adults at all levels. The laity—children and adults—are the leaders of the worship from the beginning to the end. Most Sundays, a child opens the worship service with what is called an Opening Acclamation. The priest says the prayer of consecration and the adults and very young children are both the ministers at communion: they give out the bread and the wine (with our bishop's permission), not the ordained leaders. We use a small child-sized altar, a storyteller chair, and lots of other symbols.

How to Use This Book

We offer this book because we have found that this service attracts people who are afraid of church, worried about their children in church, seekers for something new and refreshing, and because we have been asked by many to share what we are doing and what we have learned.

This book invites you to explore the theology and practice of intergenerational worship and determine how you might create such a service in your church. There are four sections:

- *Section One: Children and Worship* will share our thoughts of the theology of worshipping with children, their households, other adults and the components of our liturgy. Shawn shares how children, parents, grandparents, and other adults have embraced The Rite Place.

- *Section Two: Children and Music* explores how music is a core element of teaching faith and forms the thread that holds The Rite Place together for all ages from Dennis' perspective. Learn how you can teach music to children with simple chanting and joyful noise.

- *Section Three: The Liturgies* gives you a step-by-step look at how The Rite Place "works" with explanations for how you can create your own "Rite Place" in your congregation. This section includes our liturgies for all the seasons of the church year, written by the staff of Grace Church. A Song Book is included with all of Dennis' music compositions used at The Rite Place.

- *Section Four: Resources* offers additional ways to make your services child-inclusive. You'll find a process for discerning the creation of your own service, ways you can explore whether it is right for your congregation, and tips from how to pick out ways to proclaim the lessons, prepare a child-friendly sermon, to how to help the altar guild prepare.

Welcome to "The Rite Place."

Section One:

Children and Worship

Chapter 1:

Planting the Seeds and Taking the Plunge

> *Jesus also said, "With what can we compare the kingdom of God, or what parable will we use for it? It is like a mustard seed, which, when sown upon the ground, is the smallest of all the seeds on earth; yet when it is sown it grows up and becomes the greatest of all shrubs, and puts forth large branches, so that the birds of the air can make nests in its shade."*
>
> (Mark 4:30-32)

IN 2008 GRACE CHURCH FORMED A TASK FORCE ALONG WITH the staff and vestry to discern whether we should start a new, additional service. We were clear from the very beginning that we wanted to reach out to those who were not going to church. We wanted a service that would invite people to experience God in new and profound ways. We believed that starting a service that was already like the one we had would potentially split the congregation. We looked around and noticed that there were not many families with children present. It seemed to us that families with children would already be coming to a more formal service, if that is what they wanted. So, what would bring them into church that would fit within the Episcopal Church's liturgical style that we were not doing already?

Would this be a service just for children? What would their parents get out of this; what about their spiritual needs? Would the liturgy attract adults in addition to parents? These were just a few of the questions that members of Grace asked when they heard about the desire to offer what is now our "The Rite Place. Kids Do Church! Adults Do Too!" service.

In the Beginning

Knowing that Grace was leaning towards starting a service like the one at St. Columba's Episcopal Church, in Washington D.C., I decided to pay them a visit to see it for myself and to ask as many questions as I could. (We had not experienced the service while we were there with our Madrigal Choirs, so going and seeing it seemed to be a wise decision.) I did not tell anyone at St. Columba's that I was coming. I was hoping that a surprise visit would prompt unrehearsed answers when I asked questions.

I sat at the back of the church in order to get a full view of all that was happening. Because of some construction in the church, they were having their service in the Parish Hall. The presider (the priest who was leading the service) welcomed all and the procession started with young children carrying the cross and the torches, and then the other members of the altar party. All were in a variety of kinds of vestments. Children and adults all stayed in their seats until the gospel and sermon, when the children were invited to come up and sit at the feet of the person reading the gospel and the one giving the sermon. The preacher was great at using objects to tell the story in ways that grabbed the attention of the young children—most were under the age of four or five.

As I observed the service I was aware that I loved the energy in the room. Folks of all ages were paying attention and when they seemed to be distracted nobody gave a stare or a comment. I was also aware of some things that I knew that we would want to do differently at Grace: an altar where children could see the bread and the wine and help set the table; communion distributed by children; adults and children collecting the gift of money; vestments worn by all who were assisting in the service so that it would show that lay and ordained alike are invited to lead worship (or no vestments at all). I knew that we would want to engage the senses so that all could experiences the sights, sounds, and touch of the liturgy and have the children of Grace to be the ones who would lead as much of the liturgy as possible; there is nothing greater than hearing the voice of children praying the prayers and guiding adults in worship.

Even with the little things that we might adjust to fit the needs and style of Grace, I knew that what I was witnessing was something that could catch on. After all, there were nearly two hundred people at this service at St. Columba's. The adults and children all seemed to be fairly engaged. Just what was it about this service that drew the parents to it?

Church ended and people were filing out and there I was, a guest in their space, ready for some conversations. Slowly I started going up to people and asking them tons of questions:

- Why do you come to this service?

- What do your children think of it?

- How does the service meet your worship needs?

- What do you think your children get out of it?

- Is there anything that you would change about it?

- Anything else you want to tell me?

- Would you recommend this kind of service be offered in other churches?

More often than not, the answers were very similar:

- *"We come here because this church really cares about children being in worship."*

- *"As a parent, I have made a decision that my children come first. I need to take them to church where they can participate, where people are not staring at them for making noise, where the sermons are presented in a way that they can understand and where I can see that they feel valued."*

- *"My needs do not matter right now."*

- *"The service meets my needs in ways that I would never imagine. Watching my child fully engaged in what is happening, is what feeds me."*

- *"It seems to me that experiencing this service will help my child better understand God and worship. Coming to this one will make it easier to attend a longer service because they will know what to expect."*

- *"I love that this service is not a dumbed down service. It has all of the components to the other services."*

- *"This service helps me to better understand Episcopal worship. I can ask questions here that I would ever dream of asking at the more formal services."*

- *"This service is a parent's dream come true. We can come to church with our children and worship together."*

The people at St. Columba's appeared to be uplifted, transformed, and excited about a service that was geared towards families with younger children. Their feedback was just what we needed to take the plunge in starting our own service for families with young children and others who might want to attend. From them we heard that adults and children were both fed. We heard that part of the success of their service was that it was different from what was being offered at other times and that tended to draw a different a crowd. The people who were coming wanted their kids to be engaged in worship and to be engaged as adults themselves; they did not want dumb-downed liturgy. For many, the shorter service worked well for children who were five and under. Parents of the littlest ones did not want to send their kids to the nursery. They wanted to worship with their children so that parent and child could pray together in a church setting that offered good traditional liturgy in ways that young children could relate.

St. Columba's philosophy, "When you talk to children about God, all listen," was the inspiration that we needed. I took my experience at St. Columba's and Dennis' energy for creating a similar service to our staff, vestry, and the small group that was formed to think about what additional service might be adopted at Grace. For us, starting a service that could be marketed to households who tend to start coming to church when they have kids, seemed to aim at a great target audience. A model had been found.

Taking the Plunge

We decided to offer a few "test the market" services. Borrowing an Ash Wednesday service that Elizabeth Hammond developed for St. Anthony's-in-the-Desert in Tucson, Arizona, we embarked on the beginnings of what has proven to be a service that was needed in our area. Over fifty people came to that Ash Wednesday service and they let us know that they liked how we engaged the children and the adults in an ancient service. They loved that the kids and adults were involved together. They liked that it was child-centered and not childish. Several parents expressed that they thought it was perfect for children under the age of five who they had experienced having a hard time paying attention in the longer service; thus, making it difficult for the adults to concentrate. Their responses were just what we needed to get going.

Grace has now been offering this since 2008. Our very first service drew around 57 people. At our height (Easter services) we have had up to 135 at The Rite Place. There are some Sundays in the summer where we have twenty. Our 10:30 a.m. service can range from 75-150 people. Some of our families have chosen to go back and forth between the two services. Some have disappeared and we are beginning to investigate where they are and why they did not stay. Some families have now moved to the 10:30 a.m. more formal service. Some families are choosing to stay with the thirty-minute service.

Over the six years we have initiated some little changes. So many kids were interested in helping give out communion that finding a way to pick kids without asking some feel too left out caused us to choose aprons (having a feel of servant ministry like the deacons) as a way to show who would be giving out the bread and the wine. We chose small aprons for the bread (younger children tend to give out the bread) and larger ones for the older children who distribute the wine. Recently children as young as three have been giving out the wine, causing us to need to plan for how to better sort out which aprons go to which children. The different-sized aprons help us to quickly determine whether we have enough communion ministers. Developing a leader's binder for the children to find their leadership parts became an amazingly helpful tool. We underline the parts that they are to lead and they can then do the service with very little prompting from the adults (the independence of children is recognized and lifted up). Handing it to a volunteer at the beginning of the service helps us to be able to look to the leader throughout the entire service. In a service like this, little details matter.

Our parents have indicated that the service is just what they needed for their families to worship together. Adults without children like to come to see the many ways that all ages are invited to participate in worship. Some households with children continue to choose our more formal service. Our intention has been to continue to welcome children at all of our services.

We are still experimenting with what we do. We are aware that the needs of the parents and children may change. We wonder if folks will keep this service as their primary service or whether they will move to the longer and more formal service held later in the morning. It is still too soon to know the answers to these questions. For now, we come together each week, gathered to love and serve the Lord.

The Congregation's Response

How has this service impacted the lives of the adults? What are they getting out of it? Are they glad that we have offered this? Here is what some of the adults in our community have to say about The Rite Place:

> *From our standpoint as parents, the children's service is a critical connection for our children and the church. When we were attending adult services before coming to Grace it was clear that Sam really wanted to connect to the service, but it was beyond his grasp and attention span. He wanted to be part of it, but he felt frustrated by it. By distilling the*

liturgy into its most critical components, incorporating interactive music, and involving the children in the service, they feel a connection that they otherwise wouldn't.

—Kate and Keith

I will say that this service has provided a chance for children to have a deeper level of participation, which my son Ryan and daughter Evelyn love. Instead of Raquel and I being focused on the kids being quiet for a traditional service, the church has provided an inclusive and accessible service for them to participate in.

—Thank you for this, Christian and Raquel

The participation level for children during The Rite Place is an essential piece of our worship experience. Rather than occupying the kids for an hour or more with books, or crayons, just to get them through, and helping them focus on the service when we are able, our children are investing in the service from the beginning. They have learned from memory the short, but reflective hymns. They read and lead. They participate during communion. There is never a sense that they aren't ready, aren't good enough; never a sense that some kids are "better," "smarter," or "more able" to participate than others. Every child is good enough, ready enough, and has something to offer. When at this service, the kids are full members of the body, for the full thirty minutes, no distractions required. The added benefit of this is that we can also be fully involved. No concerns that other parishioners will judge or interfere with the children's involvement, and with kids who are involved, so are we able to fully focus on the service. —Amanda

I can't tell you how it fills my heart to see Paul reading, and knowing it enough now that it's almost memorized. I think that, in and of itself, is the most powerful example of how focused and attentive at least Paul is during the service. First, I love that the 9:00 a.m. service follows the lectionary calendar. It is one of the things that struck me when I joined the Episcopal Church. Speaking specifically about this for kids, it's important for me to know they will hear the full cycle of readings and not the kid-friendly, easy readings that are typically used for children's sermons. I'm also very happy that the message is always tied to the reading. Shawn and others do an extraordinary job of making the message engaging for the kids without removing the core message of the reading. —Noah

When we moved to Oak Park, I began looking for a church that would engage my children and help them grow spiritually. I found just what I was looking for at Grace Episcopal Church. My children and I love to attend the 9:00 a.m. family service on Sundays. The kids are not expected to sit in the pews and not speak a word, as I was expected to do as a child while in church. Instead, the kids are welcomed by Rector Shawn and the community, and encouraged to participate in the service. Both my children love to sing, recite the prayers, light the candles, and administer the Body and Blood of Christ. And all along, the community welcomes them, encourages them, and makes us all feel like we're a part of this community. I am proud to say we are a part of this loving and welcoming church community. —Cecily

I would like to share a few things about my experience with the children's service. I was raised Episcopalian. My grandchildren have come into the church recently with my daughter-in-law, Cecily. Addison and Braden have been exposed through the children's service to what worship actually is. Through participating in the ceremony first hand they fully enjoy being there. They sing "Amen, Amen" (kick it louder!) at the dinner table. I never did that as a kid. When I came and saw them participating in a way that is meaningful to them I was so thrilled. It is truly a blessing. I also believe the service benefits others to see the children participating. Thank you so much for implementing this program. I'm so glad my grandchildren are a part of it! —Andrea

Shortly after we started The Rite Place at Grace Church, we decided to do a survey as a way to engage our congregation in their input to the worship services at Grace. Some of the feedback we received:

An amazing community has formed around the 9:00 a.m. service. This has been a source of support and joy for many young families. I like how we all welcome visitors to that service and make sure that everyone feels at home. The service has a great feel to it and has done a lot to make kids feel a sense of comfort and ownership at church.

I love the 9:00 a.m. service. It is so beautiful to watch the children fully understand what is going on. I have seen toddlers toddle to the altar, watching with great delight. I think it is so important to introduce these concepts at such an early age.

In thinking about making a video of Grace, one person wrote: "I would highlight the inclusion of the children in a service … I think worship plays such a pivotal role in their development. When children feel they belong, they will keep coming back."

The first time I attended the 9:00 a.m. service I thought that it was very "cute" that young children took on the roles of Eucharistic Ministers. As I approached a boy of about seven years of age to receive the bread, he looked at his parent and said, I "forgot the word," and then quickly handed me the sacrament, looked me straight in the eyes said, "This is Jesus' body," and smiled. At that moment I was so happy to be a member of this community of true believers—young and old.

Children's worship service: I don't have children, but the one service I attended was engaging, affirming, and offered a positive foundation for growth.

Looking Forward

One of the questions we continually ask is whether the adults who come to The Rite Place are being fed spiritually. Noah's answer sums up many of their responses:

"As far as I personally am concerned, your question is difficult to answer at this point as I'm struggling a bit to know what I actually do need. What I would say now is that although I do miss the ritual and the music of the later service, I am much happier knowing that the kids are engaged and participating. This is actually good for me at this

point. I'm giving myself some space to let the kids engage and create their own thoughts. That said, the core of the service is grounded and full enough that I feel that I'm only missing the ritual and not as much the theology. I believe that when it's time for the kids to move up to the later service, the kids will be ready, and I will be ready myself to engage more with the Grace community as a whole, and possibly do choir."

Grace Church has embarked on and in an ever-unfolding journey in all of our worship services. What meets the needs of the parents and children today, may not be down the road. Our hope is that in all that we do in worship and outside of worship, we are offering encounters with God–encounters that will allow all to come away from this place wanting to be followers of the gospel and doers of the Word.

Chapter 2:

We Are the Body of Christ

> *For just as the body is one, and has many members, and all the members of the body, though many, are one body, so it is with Christ. For in the one Spirit we were all baptized into one body—Jews or Greeks, slaves or free—and we were all made to drink of one Spirit. Indeed, the body does not consist of one member, but of many.*
>
> (1 Corinthians 12:12-14)

IMAGINE THE VOICE OF A THREE-YEAR-OLD CHILD WHO IS looking up at you, offering you a piece of bread and saying, "The Body of Christ. THE BODY OF CHRIST." Now close your eyes and imagine it again. Breathe it in as you begin to believe that we are all indeed part of the Body. In that body, all people of all ages are equal, valued, gifted, and offered a role in the ministry of the Church. At Grace Church, Oak Park that includes fully participating in the worship services.

To help us put this theology into words for children and adults, we frequently sing the hymn written by Dennis: "We are all children of God, every one of every age. Father, sister, friend, brother, mother, stranger, all! We are all children of God!"

What we do in our worship on Sundays is the catalyst for how we live our lives all week. So, what does it mean to BE the Body of Christ? Why is that important for the worship that we do, the children in our midst, and the ministries that we lead?

Many people who hear the phrase, "The Body of Christ," frequently think of the bread that is given to them during a communion service. Bread that, depending on your religious expression, is believed to be the spiritual representation or actual body of Jesus Christ. On Maundy Thursday we remember Jesus washing the feet of His disciples, letting them know that the bread and wine they are sharing at his last meal with them would soon represent His body and blood, and the disciples waiting all night with Jesus in the Garden of Gethsemane is the beginning of when the Body of Christ takes on this new meaning.

> *"…the Body of Christ means not just the person of the historical Jesus and the real presence of God in the Eucharist, but also the concrete, historical body of believers on earth…. In essence, Jesus is saying: 'You cannot deal with a perfect, all-loving, all-forgiving, all-understanding God in heaven, if you cannot deal with a less-than-perfect, less-than-forgiving, and less-than understanding community here on earth.'"[1]*

---

[1] Ronald Rolheiser, *The Holy Longing: The Search for a Christian Spirituality* (New York: Doubleday, 1999), 98 and 99.

Jesus' disciples were stunned that he had washed their feet, for in their world He was the great one and they should have offered this intimate service to Him. But not our Jesus; He knew that the world was about to be different and He wanted to open the eyes of His disciples to their role in this world.

> *Jesus asked them, "Do you understand what I have done for you?" "You call me 'Teacher' and 'Lord,' and rightly so, for that is what I am. Now that I, your Lord and Teacher, have washed your feet, you also should wash one another's feet. I have set you an example that you should do as I have done for you. Very truly I tell you, no servant is greater than his master, nor is a messenger greater than the one who sent him. Now that you know these things, you will be blessed if you do them.* (John 13.12-17).

Jesus gave his disciples the bread saying, "Take and eat; this is my body." Every time we receive communion we are invited in a new way to be the Body of Christ in the world. We are invited into a way of life where we are called to live as Jesus lived, to welcome the strangers, the outcasts, the oppressed, and all of God's humanity. We are invited to wash the feet of the world.

The Rite Place service is one of our ways of inviting the church into a new way of being. It is a liturgy in which we show with our words and deeds that young children and their families are welcomed and valued in a worship environment. Welcomed in a way that invites all to lead and participate in worship. Too many congregations send a message to children that they should be seen but not heard. Not Grace. We are saying to bring yourselves, your children, and other adults into a worship where all are equal and are called to leadership. Our parish administrator, Douglas VanHouten coined our mission: "All are welcome. Period." Young, old, strong or fragile; all are part of Christ's body.

As the Body of Christ, we are reminded that our faith is an active faith. Hopefully a product of participating in worship is the ability and willingness to take what we hear in worship, what we witness in worship, and what we do in worship, outside the "structural doors" of the church and into the world of church that is our daily life.

We Will With God's Help: Our Promises at Baptisms
"Holy Baptism is full initiation by water and the Holy Spirit into Christ's Body, the Church" (*BCP*, p. 298).

Sam picks up the pitcher of water, pours it into a cup and then into a bowl. One by one all who enter follow the same action. We then sing some hymns, process to the place in the church where we listen to a part of the Great Story from the Bible, and invite those who are to be baptized, parents of the young person, and the sponsors of anyone else who will be baptized to come forward. As they stand before the assembly, or in the midst of the assembly, we dive into the Baptismal liturgy (*BCP*, p. 302-303):

> Presider: *Will you be responsible for seeing that the child you present is brought up in the Christian faith and life?*

Parents and Godparents: *I will, with God's help.*

Presider: *Will you by your prayers and witness help this child to grow into the full stature of Christ?*

Parents and Godparents: *I will, with God's help.*

Presider: *Will you who witness these vows do all in your power to support these persons in their life in Christ?*

People: *We will.*

Perhaps one of the parts that can be the most powerful is when the assembly proclaims the loud, "We will." We will support these persons in their life in Christ. We say it and then try to figure out what it really means to do that. We notice that our vow is not age-restricted. We don't promise before God, the person to be baptized, their parents and godparents, and the rest of the Body of Christ assembled: "We will until the terrible twos or until puberty or until teenage rebellion sets in at which point all bets are off." We say, "We will" without restriction. What can such support mean?

At Grace, one parishioner is the epitome of what it means to be a godparent and to assist in the raising of those she sponsors in their upbringings in faith. From spending time with her godchildren to bringing them to church to being there in joys and sorrows, she takes on the responsibility of raising good and faithful people with gusto and grace. Our own parish administrator, Douglas, has led his own congregation, the people of the Episcopal Diocese of Chicago, and Grace Church in the relentless reminder that baptism equals ministry. Ministers are not all of the sudden formed when a bishop lays his or her hands on someone at ordination. Ministers are all of us—lay and ordained.

For Episcopalians, where baptism can be offered the minute you are born into this world, your ministry, your living your faithful life starts as you leave your mother's womb. Parents, godparents, friends, family, and faith communities make a commitment at baptism (hopefully, even when someone is in the womb) to do all that we can to be present for and with the newly baptized. We promise to be role models of faith. We promise to teach and lead and form one another in our lives in Christ.

Young children need to be invited in age-appropriate ways to be ministers of the faith. They should never be given the message that they are the "future of the church." They are the church with us, right here and now, and they have their rightful place in the world and in their faith communities. What better way to keep children in church, than to invite them to engage in leadership from the earliest of ages! More than keeping them in church, we are modeling that baptism really does equal ministry.

For those not prepared to allow children to be leaders, then perhaps we should leave out the prayer that we pray after someone is newly baptized:

Give them an inquiring and discerning heart, the courage to will and to persevere, a spirit to know and to love you, and the gift of joy and wonder in all your works. Amen. (*BCP*, p. 308)

In reality, we would never leave these words out. Words register in our minds even when we do not quite understand them. Everyone at a baptism hears these words; we are praying that our children will ask questions, grow in their faith, and hopefully want to know more about what and how God's love can transform their lives.

Children as Communion Ministers

Shortly after passing the Peace and starting the Prayer of Thanksgiving over the bread and wine, two-year-old Chris walked up to the child-size altar and said, "I want to help." We watched and waited as Chris picked up the paten (plate) with the bread and started breaking the bread into small pieces. He then took his place by the chalice bearer (person with the wine) and placed the bread in the receiver's hands and said, "The Body of Christ, the Bread of Heaven." It was a holy moment.

Eric came to Grace Church as a postulant for the priesthood and he spent months observing our worship services. In reflecting on our Rite Place service and the role of children at communion, Eric was drawn to say, "The last few minutes have been a little bit of a mess. A group of children mostly tailed by parents, have been exchanging the Peace, with varying degrees of exuberance and expertise. Whether shy or outgoing, all have been mobile and the precarious stillness of the Prayers of the People is already a distant memory. It has been a blessed chaos of a few moments. Someone starts making announcements and a minimal order somehow starts emerging. Some children happily return to seats, while parents who have perfected a kind of reverent-hurried-shuffle retrieve other kids. Adults unaccompanied by children sit back just a little bit in their chairs or pews, smiles playing at the corners of their lips."

"Siblings settling down on the floor, before the small altar, exchange last whispers. Hopefully, an offering basket makes the rounds and those kids in chairs show the baffling childhood glee of giving money to the church (a glee that is less baffling when we remember that it is usually not the child's own money being tossed with such abandon into the basket).

"Finally, a small bell is rung calling us to silent prayer, in preparation for the Eucharist. A final fidget runs quickly through the gaggle of children gathered around the altar. Some have been given aprons during the announcements, designating them as assistants at the Eucharist. And then a stillness descends. This is the gathered assembly of the People of God in this place: a priest, a deacon, a musician, children, parents, friends, a couple catechists, a number of adults without children, one of the oldest saints in the congregation. Whatever it means to be the people of God, we are it here, this morning.

"The Eucharistic prayer is participatory. The presider leads with and among us, the multi-generational assembly. Children participate even in the ceremonial actions: a hundred hands stretching at the Epiclesis, tiny hands elevating the bread and wine, sometimes steadied by a parent or the deacon. Importantly, none of these actions are mimicry—they are participatory. The presider leads, and we all—the people of God—pray. After the bread and wine are consecrated and we have prayed as Our Lord taught us, an impromptu collection of adults shepherds the young ministers to their places: four younger children carry with them the consecrated bread, older children or adults carry the much trickier chalices of consecrated wine. And we all file forward in a ragged but reverent order and receive communion from the children, tiny voices saying "The Body of Christ, the Bread of Heaven," sometimes with gentle prompting from an adult hovering behind them.

"In these young assistants at communion, the Body of Christ in the Eucharist is made fresh, and the Body of Christ as the Church is expanded and renewed. Christ redeems these children, through the same redeeming work that saves the adults. We together—adults, children, parents, Presider—are all children of God and each has gifts to give to and receive from the others. The children learn responsibility and participation in the Christian life; the adults learn to encounter God in new places and to see the full Christian agency of the community's youngest members. All of us are given a larger appreciation of God's grace because of its work through these smallest members of God's Church."

Chris as a communion minister and Eric's reflection on his experience of the service are just a few of the moments when we knew that having young children as communion ministers would have a profound impact on the children and the entire assembly (congregation).

In the Catechism (*BCP*, p. 855-856) we are reminded that:

The ministers of the church are lay persons, bishops, priests, and deacons;

- The ministry of lay persons is to represent Christ and his Church; to bear witness to him wherever they may be; and, according to the gifts given them, to carry on Christ's work of reconciliation in the world; and to take their place in the life, worship, and governance of the Church;

- The duty of all Christians is to follow Christ; to come together week by week for corporate worship; and to work, pray, and give for the spread of the kingdom of God.

- The children of Grace are being formed from birth in the understanding that they have a valuable place in the life and ministry of the Episcopal Church, and that includes the ministry of a Lay Eucharistic Minister in our worship services. We adopted this position because of our understanding that ministry starts at birth. Thankfully, Jeffrey Lee, Bishop of the Episcopal Diocese of Chicago, is a firm believer in bringing formation and worship to life in profound and sometimes new ways. He understands that structures and policies of the Church are changing and that there is a deep need to think outside of the box. Early on in his tenure he proclaimed that we should, "Form the Faithful, Grow the Church, and Change the World."[2] The ministry of the children is doing just that.

---

[2]   http://www.episcopalchicago.org/our-diocese/the-bishop/bishop-lee/ (Accessed March 18, 2014).

The Lord IS With You.

The Lord be with you! And also with you! Across the world, congregations begin the table prayer (Eucharistic prayer, the prayer of consecration of the bread and wine) and other prayers with a variation of this ancient opening acclamation (salutation, opening words) between the leader of the prayers (typically a priest) and assembly (congregation).

Not at Grace. "The Lord IS with You! The Lord IS also with You!" That is what echoes through our church every single Sunday. We decided to make the statement that the Lord is already with us. Praying it the other way makes us sound as if the Lord may or may not be with us.

If we are completely honest, we will admit that when we first suggested using our alternative, people were not at all happy that we would be messing with words that are so ancient. We persevered in proclaiming, "The Lord is with You" in our Rite Place liturgy and temporarily gave up the idea of using it for any of our other services.

In her book, *Taste and See: Savoring the Child's Wisdom,*[3] Pam Moore, a catechist (leader and teacher) with *Catechesis of the Good Shepherd*[4] (a Montessori-based Christian formation program) describes how in her early years of working with children she would find pieces of paper or be handed pieces of paper that said, "Mrs. Moore, the Lord is with you." She was pleased that the children were growing in their understanding and awareness of God that she was providing. In reflecting back on those years, Pam began to wonder if the children were letting her know that God was already in her work. What a beautiful gift they gave her. The Lord IS with you, Mrs. Moore.

God is in the now. Jesus is in the now. That is exactly why we use those words in our service. Children live in the now. We want them and the adults to hear and know that the Lord IS working in and around us right here and right now. Pam Moore came to realize that children frequently will say that the Lord is already with us. They just know it.

Can you imagine a world where people grow up exposed to the truth that the Lord is in our laughter, our tears, our work, our play, our family, our schools and heaven help us, in our worship and in our churches? The Lord is present in the here and now. Thanks be to God!

---

[3]   Pam Moore, *Taste and See: Savoring the Child's Wisdom* (Chicago: Catechesis of the Good Shepherd Publications, 2012)..

[4]   http://www.cgsusa.org

Chapter 3:

Liturgy as Formation

> *The wolf shall live with the lamb, the leopard shall lie down with the kid, the calf and the lion and the fatling together, and a little child shall lead them.*
>
> (Isaiah 11:6)

A GROUP OF CHILDREN GATHERED IN THE PARISH HALL FOR A question-and-answer period with Bishop Jeffrey Lee, for the diocesan event, *Come Children Sing*. Jeff, dressed in the full "bishop uniform"—clerical collar, purple shirt, pectoral cross, cassock and surplice, cope, and miter—spent time explaining much of what he was wearing and answering any question that was asked. After hearing comments about baptism, one child raised a hand and asked, "Why are we anointed with oil at our baptism?" I could not see who the child was, but I was impressed with the depth of the question.

At the core of The Rite Place is the desire to create an atmosphere to explore these questions from and with the children. Sunday after Sunday we attempt to break open those deep questions with the congregation for further exploration. I say, "with the congregation" because our style is not to preach at or talk *to*, but to preach and talk *with* one another.

The questions may come from the hymn they just sang, at the blowing of the shofar[1] when they pick up the seasonal object[2] for the procession, during the prayers, while setting the table, during the taking up of the offering of money, while giving out communion, during or after the reading of the lessons or the mostly interactive sermon that was preached, etc.

Our own passion and the actions of the Episcopal Church's General Convention[3] are certainly a part of our drive in creating The Rite Place. The Reverend Canon Robyn Szoke-Coolidge, former Children's Ministry Officer for the Episcopal Church, gives some of the best background and support for offering unique opportunities in worship and other formation offerings for children and their families:

---

[1]   The shofar, the horn of a ram or a goat or a sheep, is mostly familiar to us these days from the Jewish tradition, especially for its many trumpetings at the New Year's festival of Rosh haShanah. Its roots go back further, into Biblical times, and it's from some of these usages that we borrow. The human breath blowing through the horn and producing that loud noise reminds us of the One who first breathed into the first human beings, inviting them to life (Genesis 2:7). The word is used for the first time in the Bible to introduce those who would become the People of God to the God who was claiming them, at Mount Sinai (Exodus 19:13,16). It was the shofar that summoned the People of God to holy assembly (e.g. Numbers 29:1); it accompanied the ark of the covenant—a potent symbol for our ancestors of the intentional presence of God in their midst—in procession (Chronicles 15:28); it announced and celebrated the presence of God as ruler (Psalm 98.6).

[2]   When you look at our liturgies in Section Three, you will see that all participants are invited to carry in a seasonal object as they enter church. For Advent through Epiphany there are small battery operated lights; small wooden crosses for Lent; bells in Eastertide; and a variety of things for the summer. We find these symbols/objects to be small ways to bring different images for the different seasons of the church year. At the end of our procession we place a small basket to collect what is carried in as a small way to help prevent the struggles of little kids not quite knowing how to share.

[3]   The General Convention is the governing body of the Episcopal Church that meets every three years to debate and act on legislation that sets the Church's priorities for mission.

Looking back, it seems that the theology of the 1979 *Book of Common Prayer* helped to launch a grassroots mission movement for advocacy with and ministry to (and for and by) children. [We] began to engage in deeper conversations about how best to serve children, including how best to fully include them in our worship communities and the prophetic notion of listening and hearing their voice.

The result of these conversations saw the adoption of *The Children's Charter for the Church* at General Convention in 1997. It provides a model—a standard of excellence—and accountability for congregational, diocesan, and provincial leadership . . . .

Importantly, the 2003 church-wide conference, *Will Our Faith Have Children* included children, uplifting their voices. In doing so, the conference challenged the community to include children as full members. Indeed, the full inclusion of children into the worshiping community, the formational community, and the mission community became a central goal [of the Episcopal Church].[4]

The leadership of the Episcopal Church gave churches across the country the courage to dream about what could be for and in the life of children. They publicly declared and challenged congregations to boldly live into supporting children in their lives of faith—promises we make at all baptisms.

Informed by Baptism

Give them an inquiring and discerning heart, the courage to will and to persevere, a spirit to know and to love you, and the gift of joy and wonder in all your works. Amen. (BCP, p. 308)

It seems to me the best way to convey the impact of our service on and in the life of our children is to share some stories that embody the prayer that we say following the action of the water pouring upon the newly baptized.

An Inquiring and Discerning Heart

Sunday after Sunday I find myself learning from the children. They get me to think about things that I have never thought or at least have not considered in the ways they prompt. Their opening up and asking questions that some of the rest of us would never dare, is their way of helping to lead and form us. They are the teachers and the learners.

Sam helps remind us that we all learn in different ways. Some of us are visual learners, some are oral learners and some are both. He told his parents, "I like walking around the church and looking at the Bible stories that are told in the windows."

The Courage to Will and to Persevere

It is Communion time and a new member volunteers to give out the bread and is not quite sure where to go and stand to give the bread to others. A child whispers, "Don't be nervous, follow me and I'll show you where to stand and what to say."

---

[4] "Ministry with Children in the Episcopal Church" http://buildingthecontinuum.wordpress.com/2012/03/31/ministry-with-children-in-the-episcopal-church/ Accessed March 6, 2014.

An adult was asked if they wanted to be the leader of the worship that day and I could see the look of terror in his eyes. Their son took the leader's book and said, "Don't worry, I can show you what to do. It is pretty cool being the leader and nobody will care if you make a mistake."

Paul describes being the worship leader in this way, "Leading the service is very fun and gives you a chance to learn why the service is set up the way it is, and it helps kids focus on who and what the service is about. "

We Will With God's Help.

That is how we announce that we will do all in our power to support each baptized person in his or her life of faith. In many ways we promise to help them have inquiring minds that will seek and serve Christ in all that they do, loving their neighbors as themselves, giving them the will to persevere and the excitement to know, serve and love God in all that they and we do. If we offer even the slightest glimpse of this in our worship and formation lives, the world will be a better place, we will be better people because of children being grounded in the heart of the gospel message to love and serve all. They will be able to—wait a minute, they already are—be formed with the knowledge that they are valued by humanity and by God. That, my friends, is what it means to grow up in the Christian faith and life.

A Spirit to Know and to Love You

We had just processed down the center of the church when a two-and-a-half-year-old boy places his cross in the basket and plops himself down right in the center of the carpet. Soon, the gospel is being read and as in many typical Sundays, people are arriving late and walking down that same aisle. He turns and says, "Come on in. You're not late. You can sit right here." He did not shame anyone. A simple message of welcome was what he offered. "Do not neglect to show hospitality to strangers, for by doing that some have entertained angels without knowing it." (Hebrews 13:2)

Another child supplies for our musician when he is away and boldly gathers us to begin the singing before the service. She tells the assembly not to worry about whether they can sing or not because God does not care.

The priest breaks the bread and a young one says, "I think that is the most important part. It is my favorite part."

When asked to say something about the service, young Peter shared, "I like giving peace to everyone. Peace is love." Somehow he knows that exchanging the Peace is not just about greeting each other and asking about how your day is or sharing a favorite toy. Passing the Peace is about bringing the love back into a relationship that might be broken. It is about bringing the love of Christ to another person. Peter proclaims, "God is someone who loves in our hearts."

And a Gift of Joy and Wonder in All Your Works

Children are so open to wonder about what is being done around them and they are rarely shy about asking. One child reminded us that we had not changed the color for the new season and that the bulletin for Epiphany had been placed out instead of the one for Lent.

One child raised her hand and said, "I wonder if the picture of the Good Shepherd was the same Good Shepherd in the story that we just heard and the deacon read."

Unexpected Revelations

"My teaching is not mine but his who sent me." (John 7:16)

After five years of sharing in the leadership of this service, I have noticed several things that I would never have expected. I love that:

- a six-month-old turns at the sound of bell,

- the rain stick draws the smallest to pay attention to the action,

- a crawler begins to wander over to the child-sized altar,

- a two-year-old walks to the altar to carry the bread to the people,

- a six-year-old helps the two year old break the bread,

- an eighteen-month-old engages the hand motions to the yet unknown verbally articulated words to the song,

- one who is getting restless will make the decision by herself to move over to the soft space to interact with whatever it is they need that day,

- parents are fairly patient with the restlessness of children,

- someone who is just learning to walk goes to get the offering baskets and walks around to collect the gift of money,

- a parent steps in to help set the table when our deacon is away,

- a child will start laughing when I forget the Lord's Prayer, and

- a child realizes that they are now big enough to carry the chalice of wine.

There is something quite profound when you see the look in someone's eyes just right as they have an "aha" moment, when they seem to get a new understanding of something that they have been doing week after week.

I think she had been coming for a little over a year. She had watched the aprons being put on the other children and seemed to never care about that. One Sunday, she walked up to me and took an apron from my hand, asked me to put it on her, went and sat down by the child-sized altar and began to help the deacon prepare the table. When the Eucharistic prayer was over she picked up the small bowl with the bread in it and toddled over to the communion station and waited for people to come. When no one came right away, she whispered in a voice that I could barely hear, "Come on up, Jesus is ready." WOW!

I also love the time when one young child had finished giving out Communion and took the towel back to the altar table. Her mother, knowing that the chalice and cloth were to go over on a different table, went to stop her. I convinced her to wait and watch. Her daughter was resetting the table like she had done with the deacon earlier. Watching. They are always watching.

There is so much more that could be shared. I can say that I no longer worry when I hear a young bread giver notice that someone has missed the chalice of wine and says with a loud voice, "You want some tea?" Soon that very child will know and understand in a new way that the liquid in the glass is actually the Blood of Christ. For now, the child knows that someone just missed out on something important.

We are called to support and nourish and nurture our children in their lives of Christ. The Rite Place is just one of many ways that Grace Church attempts to do just that. The service is not perfect, it is not always quiet, and it is sometimes hard to know whether we have reached the children and the adults. It is, however, one of the best examples I have ever shared in the leadership of helping our children to grow in the full stature of Christ.

Section Two:

Children and Music

Chapter 4:

Singing Our Story

> *Be joyful in the Lord, all you lands; serve the Lord with gladness and come before his presence with a song.*
>
> Psalm 100:1 (Jubilate Deo, *BCP*, p. 729)

MUSIC CENTERS. MUSIC FOCUSES. MUSIC PUTS A POINT ON A concept. Music allows words of faith to linger in one's mind and heart. Music washes over you. When we sing, we tell our story. In song, we tell who we are, and who we are not. We proclaim what is important to us. We name things that are of interest to us. We pose moral situations, question ideas and use song to celebrate special occasions.

Many books have been written on church music on why singing is so important. The book of Psalms is an example of how music has been (and continues to be) central to God's people in their worship. The English word "psalm" is derived from a Greek word, which in turn translates a Hebrew word meaning "musical praise." I frequently teach groups that, in a way, the Psalter is an extended and seemingly private conversation between the psalmist and God. If you read it, you see there are no doubts about God's existence, and only few doubts that God is hearing absolutely everything the psalmist is bringing up. We, when reading the book, are listening in on a private conversation. The Psalmist expresses a huge array of emotions in the Psalms: not only mad, glad, sad, bad, but also the feelings of exultation, despondency, frustration, and even incomprehension!

We read in Psalm 100:1, "Be joyful in the Lord, all you lands; serve the Lord with gladness and *come before his presence with a song.*" Over and over again in the Psalter, singing is linked with worship of God. Singing is a thing we do to address God. Throughout the Old Testament, when the children of God gathered, they sang their story. They also sang their praises. It cannot be overstated how deep a connection goes between worship and song.

Have you ever had the experience of singing a rousing closing hymn at a Eucharist with a congregation, and then found yourself later that day or later that week humming the tune or singing the first verse? The discipline of walking the Christian walk is difficult, and requires real commitment; but the words of faith on wings of song can support us on our journey. It also connects us with our own soul.

Music is central in these services and sets the tone of worship. It can also be a way to move the collective in an emotional direction. If the Sunday is a rambunctious one, before the reading of the Gospel we sing, "Draw us to your center, O Lord" or "Lord, give us time of quiet stillness, give us peace" and the room often perceptively calms down. On a rather sleepy Sunday, after the sermon and prayers are finished, to add life to the service we sing, "Stir up the flame" and then we share the peace with smiles and joy! "Help us, O Lord to be your eyes. Help us, O Lord, to be your voice. Help us, O Lord to be your smile. Help us, O Lord, to be your love in all the world!" frames for all in the congregation, not just children, how we are commissioned to be to a broken world.

Music in The Rite Place teaches things directly. "We are the family tree of God" or "We are all children of God, everyone of every age, father, sister, friend, brother, mother, stranger, all" identify us as a community gathered. "Peace, my friend, I wish for you," allows a person to interact musically, and in a sense, bless another other with peace. Songs frame the liturgical seasons by describing them. "Tell the Watchman the King is Coming" says Advent in the same way as "Halleluia! Christ is Risen Again!" proclaims Easter. "Light to scatter the darkness" in Advent or Epiphany points to the importance of the symbolism around light in both of these seasons. "Jesus there is darkness without you; come into our hearts and shed your light. Help us love the world as you would do; trying every day to live just right" uses the imagery of light and darkness; a very real and deep understanding to even our youngest worshippers. In the same way, "Prepare the way for the King! Prepare the way for Jesus! Prepare the way for the King! Prepare the way for the Lord!" gets us in the spirit of the Palm Procession immediately at the outset of the service.

There are two other reasons to sing in these services. With children and their families there needs to be playfulness to worship. "Bless the birds and beasties too! Bless the cats, and dogs and bears; you know God loves them and you. Knows you joys your fears your cares. God loves you!" or in the song "These are all a gift from God! _____ are a gift from God! Halleluia!" We playfully insert into the blank: brothers, sisters, mothers, fathers, children, teachers, pastors, leaders, babies, kitties, doggies, critters, grannies, grandpas, aunties, or uncles. It is great fun and the people love it. It is also important to sing songs in foreign languages. Children are open to this; it is adults who are hesitant. In the service we can sing "Jubilate Deo" (O be joyful in the Lord) or *Hiney ma tov* (how good and pleasant it is for all to dwell together).

Who Should Sing?

Everyone should sing! We should all sing as if our (eternal) lives depend on it! It does! These words of the songs contained here, set to music, should "stick to the ribs" of your soul. Sing out! Try it—you will like it!

For the past five years we have observed the children participating, praying, and singing while some parents simply watch. This sends messages that probably are not intentional, but the children pick up on them. Subliminally it says, "We will watch you little kids do this silly thing while we sit back and relax." Encourage adults to participate gently, as singing also forms a sense of community—and they are as much of this community as the children. As a leader in this service it is important to invite everyone of every age to participate. Good singing, vibrant singing requires a little effort. To sing with fervor requires fervor!

Singing with Children

I have spent over forty years working with children and children's choirs. You will find books that state factually that a young child's voice has a limited and low range and can barely span an octave from middle C on a piano to the C above. Nothing could be farther from the truth! Children, even three-year-olds, possess beautiful voices with significant ranges. In our services, I pitch the songs on the high side. Children easily join in! Avoid pitching songs too low to make it comfortable for the cantor or for the adults. Good singing, well-supported singing takes wing in a very different way from unsupported, un-energetic mumbling of song.

Writing New Songs

Why write new songs? Songs of faith are catechetical. Here I have tried to put virtues on the wings of melody. Remember, music lingers. Hence, the truths encapsulated in these songs are seeds of faith and Christian behavior. These songs are in no way to "dumb down" our day-to-day relationship with God and our Christian community; instead they are meant to clarify and name important components of our life of faith.

This body of song came along when these services were begun. In searching for songs for the service, we found songs that either had too many words in them, (this would eliminate participation of the very young children who are pre-literate) or had words that would not be meaningful to a young person of faith. Large piles of "fancy" words like: atonement, justification, oblation, and inaccessible, could make a song incomprehensible to a young participant. There is nothing inherently wrong with beautiful, theologically complicated texts, but their use in a service like this would disenfranchise our young constituency. If one cares for these young souls, one should take time to struggle with the texts to give immediacy and clarity to the theological concepts you are trying to present. Hence, these songs are a component of hospitality. These songs, easily learned, invite immediate participation by everyone!

When we sing we tell our story. That is central to the core of my being. My lifetime's main job is to help every person I encounter to sing his or her own song! But, what if they do not have a song? Then, it is my job to walk with them in life as they compose their song. A child's life story is continually in a state of growth; each day it gets richer, each day it gets more profound. Their story is their song.

Chapter 5:

Making Music

> *Clap your hands, all you peoples; shout to God with loud songs of joy.*
> (Psalm 47:1-3)

IF I WANTED TO WRITE A SONG, HOW WOULD I BEGIN? THERE are two obvious initial sources of texts that can be easily accessed: (1) a search for texts that form us as to how we should live and (2) listening to the voice of your heart's own ponderings. A third source would be the needs of the liturgical year and the parts of the Mass. Here are some examples of all these approaches.

Is there a text that comes from the Bible or a moral example with which you wish to present to young children? For example, "It is more blessed to give than to receive" might be a text that a child might relate to. I will later use this example to help you write a song on that text. Might a passage from the Beatitudes or Psalm 23 be immediately understandable to a child? "The Lord is my Shepherd" or "Blessed are the pure in heart for they shall see God" would be words or phrases that can be woven into a song.

Have you listened to what your heart longs for? There might be a song in there! Does your heart long for peace? Do you wish for peace for the world, or personal peace, or peace that passes understanding? Put these into words, then, we will weave them into a song. Is justice something that gives you life? Sing about it! Do you wish to give the poor and hungry bread? Do it in a song. If you care about it, you can write a song about it, and teach it to children. You are not only giving your thoughts, but your Christian perspective on living life. What calling could be higher than that?

Another place that is a wellspring of texts for children is the liturgical year. We recently celebrated All Saints' Day. Would it not be beautiful to present young minds with the text, "Blessed are the dead who die in the Lord, for they rest from their labors"? Advent, with its spirit of preparation and anticipation couched in terms of the coming light, might suggest a song on, "Come, O Light, into our hearts and homes." The story of the life of Jesus, presented in Epiphany, could open one to the concept of miracles, not just the ones He did, but miracles in our own time. Finally, there are songs with the flavor of various traditions. From the Mennonite tradition, the text "I owe the LORD a Morning song" might be a way to sing at the beginning of a new day.

The liturgy itself suggests songs. When we were designing the service at Grace, it was important to me to have the children sing the *Sanctus* or Holy, Holy, Holy. We, however, wanted them to deeply understand the text. Our staff did some theological reflection and found that "Lord you are holy, you are a God of power, your glory is everywhere. Hosanna in the highest!" covers the text exactly, but it is completely comprehensible to young minds. As the deacon or priest is preparing the table with the assistance of the young people, a song of preparation would be an effective accompaniment: "prepare our souls for food, prepare our souls with wine, help then us all, to become good and at your table dine."

A quick word here about choosing texts that do not either speak down to children or using images that may not be the best for young people. Children often get the message that they are not old enough to understand a concept or they are not ready. Again, hospitality would say that songs should invite wonder! It might be better for a child if God is not referred to as Father, but as God. Aside from the body of mystical literature that points to the Father-ness and Mother-ness of God, gender stereotypes of a male God, as an example, may not be the best first impression.

Song Writing Made Easy

To begin to compose a melody, realize that largely in Western music, we have a seven note *diatonic* scale: do, re, mi, fa, sol, la, and ti. Music is always imbued with patterns and balance. If one portion of a melody ascends, it might be balanced by the next portion of the melody, descending. If there is a grouping of notes that reads do-re-mi, that can become a *sequence* that reads do-re-mi, re-mi-fa, mi-fa-sol. These two tidbits can be a great resource when composing a song for children.

Much of music is a stepwise movement. Songs more often move in *conjunct* gestures (i.e. do-re-mi or fa-sol-la). If a song moves in leaps, the larger the leap, the less often it generally occurs. If a song starts with a large leap up, say do to la, then the rest of the melody will often wind down to where it began. A large leap in music is powerful and characteristic, so use them when composing these songs judiciously.

If you have written a text, it is time to listen carefully to your text. Listen to the rhythm inherent in the words. A text like, "Walk in the ways of God" will be our example. Some syllables are inherently longer than others. Some words are less important, and because of this, one might move through them more quickly. The above text, if you repeat it over and over might be heard as long/short/short/long/short/long; it could also be heard long/short/short/long/long/long. Another way to hear it would be to think of the important words as stronger ones; then it might be strong/weak/weak/strong/weak/strong. Here is how this would be notated in 4/4 time:

The rhythm of the texts can also give us an insight toward what meter might be appropriate for a song. The previous text would also lend itself to ¾ time. If so, it would look like this:

The text, if repeated and played with, will eventually settle down into a meter. If it seems to resist, then simply work gently with the words. Here, if we add one word, "Walk in the ways of our God" a more, what one might say, regular alternation comes to the fore and we get two pairs of long/short/short in a row before the final word.

Let's go back to the text I suggested earlier, "It is more blessed to give than to receive." Read the text. The first two words are *anacrusic*, that is, they have no direction in themselves but lead to a stronger word. One can read the text as, "it is *more* blessed" or, "it is more *blessed*." Either way the anacrusic notes lead the listener on. If we do the first one, we might use two "do's" and then leap to la for the word more. (Do, la is the interval in the song "my Bonnie lies over the ocean.")

Try your hand at writing songs for children. If you want a very inexpensive music notational program that will cost you all of ten dollars, go to www.finalenotepad.com and download the program. It is easy and actually fun to use. Below you will find a supply of texts that might have meaning to you.

Texts you might consider:

Open me to your presence.

Lead me, Lord.

Walk in the ways of God.

Be still and know that I am God.

Fill me, Lord, with your love.

Lord, you are LOVE.

I owe the LORD a Morning song (from the Mennonite tradition)

All shall be well and all shall be well and all manner of things shall be made well. (Julian of Norwich)

When you sing you tell your story. Other people cannot always name or articulate what you have experienced. There may not be a song about gerontology, or struggling with cancer, or being hurt by a very sharp word. Therefore, we need you. We need you to write and compose a song to help all of us grow as people and as a community to understand a specific aspect of this walk of faith that we all share. It is almost your responsibility to add your life experience in song.

I was the musician in a national church formation conference called NOT "Will Our Children Have Faith?" but instead, "Will Our Faith Have Children?" Our faith will have children if we all pitch in and sing them their (and our) story.

Section Three:

The Liturgy

Chapter 6:

A Practical Guide to Walking Through the Liturgy

OUR SERVICE BULLETIN LOOKS A BIT DIFFERENT THAN THE TYPICAL BULLETIN OF a Rite I or Rite II Eucharist. We follow "An Order for Celebrating the Holy Eucharist" found in the *Book of Common Prayer* (p. 400-409). In offering workshops throughout the Episcopal Church on *The Rite Place*, we receive many questions: "These ideas sound great, but I have no idea where to start?" "How did you figure out what words to use?" "Wow! This is so accessible. You really shy away from insider/outsider language." "Tell me about the sidebars."

Over the next few pages you will find an explanation of each part of the liturgy on the left page, with a view of the service on the right page. You'll learn more about why we do what we do, as well as the actions and tools (musical instruments, crosses, aprons, baskets, and more) that make the liturgy so participatory and inclusive for all ages and abilities.

Join us as we take you on a journey to the practical side of offering a new worship service, particularly one geared towards parents and their children and others who want to come along.

The Rite Place

Hospitality:

A few notes that describe who we are before the service begins:

(1) We have our full contact information on all public documents and our website is clearly displayed on banners and ads. Guests may take this material and information with them. These are potential opportunities to make connections with those who might have been touched by our liturgy and would want to contact us later.

The Rite Place

Eastertide

Grace Episcopal Church
924 Lake Street, Oak Park, Illinois 60301
708-386-8036 www.graceoakpark.org

(1) Shawn M. Schreiner, Rector shawnschreiner@sbcglobal.net

Welcome to Grace Church!

On Sundays, we have two distinct liturgies (services). Both include the Eucharist (Communion).

The first liturgy, at 9:00 am, is specifically designed for children and all in their households. Children (and adults) are active participants in an informal and relaxed setting wherein children are celebrated just as they are. We strive to build a community where all feel a sense of hope and compassion from a church that welcomes all of God's children.

The second liturgy, at 10:30 am, is a sung Eucharist and more formal in nature. Being a liturgical church, we seek to use the gifts of many—lay and ordained—in liturgical roles. We strive for engaging and thought-provoking preaching, and excellent music. On any given Sunday, our congregational singing is enhanced by one of our Children's Choirs, our Madrigal Youth Choir, or our Adult Choir.

Adults and children are welcome at all services at Grace! We encourage you to try both services and see which best fits your needs.

(2) Background regarding the service they are about to experience is also presented. Of course, first time worshippers may not read all of this before the service, however, if touched by the service, the interested person might wish to read a bit more about this place and this gathering of the People of God.

This service has been a magnet for seekers. In this context, insider versus outsider terminology i.e. using "deacon" versus "teacher" or "presider" versus "leader" immediately points up to a guest that they are not in the "in" crowd and thus are foreign. We bend over backward to welcome and to explain. It is an important form of hospitality.

(3) We characterize the liturgical season. We give background to the setting and to the season.

(4) Symbols are located throughout the liturgy that show movement and action. This is helpful to small children and visual learners as well as pointing to the shifts in the service.

Grace Church—The Rite Place ②

We are a church who firmly believes that all of God's children are welcome at the table of God. The liturgy is at the heart of all we do at Grace Church. From the full services on Sundays, to weekdays and the great feasts and seasons in the church year, we reach deeply into the riches of our Anglican tradition, building on it to explore new ways to give glory to God in our prayer and preaching and music.

We, like many others, find that when you speak directly to children, everyone listens. In this service, the teaching, the songs and the prayers will be aimed at the hearts and minds of our youngest worshippers, and all will learn something each week about the God who loves us.

We pray that this experience will be a wonderful way to connect adults with young children, and young children with adults. We strive to build a community where all feel a sense of hope and compassion from a church that welcomes all of God's children.

Please feel free to contact our rector, Shawn Schreiner, with any questions.

Eastertide

③ "Christ is risen! He is risen indeed!" This is what we shout and this is what we believe! We are Easter people! Jesus suffered, died and rose from the dead. Jesus loves us so very much he gave everything for us. We, loved by Jesus Christ, wish to reach out to the world in love. Each of us can make a difference in the world; we can make it a better place. We gather to pray and praise and then we go out into the world rejoicing in our friendship and in the love of Christ. "Christ is risen! He is risen indeed!"

Watch for these symbols and meanings: ④

Procession

Shofar

Music

Crosses

Bell

Prayer

Bible Readings

Communion

Welcome & Dismissal

Holy Spirit

Gathering:

We begin at the entrance of the church and, before the service actually commences, we sing some songs that will be sung in the service. This is an informal time. We find that this is a wonderful time to bring the community together—for guests and members to begin to form community. It is our time to nestle into what we are about to do together. Children love, absolutely love, absolutely love repetition. When it is time to worship, the song leader (Dennis) says to the Presider, "Shawn (or whom ever it is), is it time?"

(5) Over and over throughout the service we identify that it is more than acceptable to be a seeker and that, indeed, we are all seekers on various points of our faith journey.

(6) Sidebar boxes! We approach this Rite III prayer book service with the assumption that more information will help those who have questions about what they are experiencing. We do a lot with sidebar boxes and you are welcome to use these if you wish to create your own for your own liturgical space and practice.

(7) We want the service to touch all the senses if possible; taste, touch, hear, see, and smell. The sounding of a ram's horn (shofar) gathers us and says clearly, "It is time to start." Kids, by the way, love it!

(8) Over the years we have worked hard to make use of as many images of God as we can! If one looks at scripture there are many names for the persons of the Trinity: Lamb, Dove, Savior, Father, Creator, Shepherd, Comforter, and the list goes on! If you translate some from the original Greek or Hebrew you can get others, hence we use here "wind" from "*pneuma.*" Different names for God provide us different ways for us to think of her! We strive to have a young person or parent in the congregation lead the service; more about this later.

Processionals:

(9) It is what Episcopalians do! What does it mean? Simply it is an elegant way to get everyone to his or her correct places. Involving children in procession will give them a context for this throughout their lives. We give objects for all to carry in our processions for each liturgical season. You do need to make sure they are not too small for young mouths (into which everything goes!) We use small battery operated candles in Advent, wooden crosses in Lent (that the children have painted themselves), brass bells at Easter, etc. There is a collection basket at the crossing (before the altar) where we will actually sit down, and the lights, crosses, or bells are returned there at the end of the procession so that they will not distract the children throughout the liturgy.

(10) We change the Collect for each season, and try to use language that would make a young hearer engage in what we are doing.

(5) **We gather with our questions as spiritual seekers on a journey.**

We gather to find God.

A Gathering Time

Welcome

(6) We gather in the name of the God three-in-one or the Triune God, at the entrance to the church. We say hello to God and one another. We take time to see and welcome our neighbor.

We prepare.

Sounding of the Shofar (7)

Israel used the ram's horn, called a shofar, to call together the people of God.

Member or Presider of the Assembly: We gather in the name of the Creator, the Shepherd, and the Wind. Alleluia! Christ is risen! **(8)**
Assembly: The Lord is risen Indeed. Alleluia!

Opening Song

We sing a gathering song and process down the center aisle.

The Procession **(9)**

Please feel free to carry an instrument, streamer, cross, or candle as we walk down the aisle. Place these objects in the wicker baskets when we approach and surround the table.

We Begin to Pray
The Collect of the Day **(10)**

This prayer is called the Collect. The Leader or Priest "collects" or "gathers" the themes of the lesson, the church season, and the congregation into one prayer.

Member or Presider of the Assembly: God is with you.
Assembly: God is also with you.

Member or Presider of the Assembly: Let us pray.

Jesus, we gather because you rose from the tomb and you save us! By your Holy Spirit, strengthen and care for us as children of the Resurrection. **Amen**.

(11) Often this will be a quiet song to center hearts that have sung and processed. It is an opportunity to calm the mood and make it reflective for hearing the lesson and the homily.

(12) We have a storytelling chair for whoever reads or tells the bible story. The person unpacking that lesson in the homily may also choose to sit in the storyteller chair.

As this service is only thirty minutes, we have gone to one lesson. If you actively read the three-year cycle of lessons, you will see the Sunday's theme is just as easily understood in one of the first two lessons as it is in the Gospel. Further, there are some biblical texts that are distinctly not for young ears. The preacher will determine which text seems to be the one that will be for the hearers on that day.

(13) We have a number of Gospel acclamations we use throughout the year. We do not sing them once, but three times. For the younger congregants, they might not be focused yet enough to sing it the first time, but by the third time will be able to participate. Here the emphasis is on hospitality again.

(14) Our homilies are seldom longer than five minutes. The preacher is challenged to bring the Word of God to all ages. Sundays can vary widely regarding energy levels of the kids and participation. There are Sundays bristling with energy from the children and other Sundays, where, the mood is often quiet and reflective. To adequately dialogue with this group of worshippers, you have to be ready to go in directions you did not plan if you ask them leading questions!

(15) This is not actually a bell, but a singing bowl. Typically, it is a Buddhist singing bowl. You can find them on the Internet. If struck gently and crisply it has a beautiful and lingering sound. We have gotten in the habit of being still until we no longer hear the bell sound. Believe it or not, the vast majority of the time it calms the room down beautifully! The silence is almost palpable.

The Word of God: God Speaks.
We Listen and Respond.

We sing ⑪

(The song will be announced.)

 ⑫

A Story from the Hebrew Bible (Old Testament) or New Testament

Reader: Hear what the Spirit is saying to God's people.
Assembly: Thanks be to God.

or

Deacon: The Good News about Jesus as told by

_____.

Gospel Refrain
Assembly:

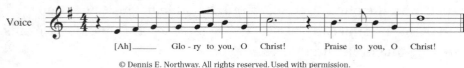

Voice

[Ah]_____ Glo - ry to you, O Christ! Praise to you, O Christ!

After the Gospel, the Deacon says: This is the Good News of the Good Shepherd.

We sing the *Gospel Refrain* again. ⑬

Homily ⑭

The sound of the bell calls us to a moment of silence.
⑮

The Old Testament is also known as the Hebrew Bible, and contains the books that were written before Jesus was born. The New Testament contains the Gospels and Epistles (letters) and the Book of Acts written by a person who knew about Jesus.

The Deacon (or someone else) tells us the story found in the Gospel appointed for this Sunday of the Church Year. This reading is always from one of four books, Matthew, Mark, Luke or John found in the Bible.

We talk about the scripture reading and what it means for us and how we live our lives.

(16) As often as we can, we strive for a literate young person to lead the intercessions (prayers). When not possible, an adult from the congregation leads the prayers. A young regular attendee of the service quickly gets the rhythm of leading this portion of the service—often faster than an adult!

The Peace, Announcements, and Offertory:

(17) This is a fairly extended component of the service. As it is concluding, some young people walk among the congregation with the offering baskets and the table begins to be prepared. The initial preparation of the table is hand sanitizer or a bowl of water and cloth for the kids and adults who eventually break the bread into bite-size pieces.

The hand sanitizing and ritual of cleaning ones' hands continues as the weekly announcements are being made. Each person who makes an announcement identifies himself or herself by name, first and always! Also, at this point, people who will distribute the bread are donning aprons and those who distribute the wine put on different aprons. Parents often help in this activity. (Curious about the aprons? You will read about that in other parts of this book.)

This offertory sentence is actually prayed after the gathering and bringing of the gifts of money and announcements have concluded. It is an initial piece to again center the gathering. If one thinks that money, bread, wine, and song are all oblations, then, this is not after the act but during!

(18) As we sing a preparation song, the elements are laid out and the chalice filled with wine and water. The children who will be the communion ministers and some parents have all settled around the table and we are about to begin the service of the table.

(19) The song should generally be quiet and reflective.

(20) The bell (singing bowl) calls us again to quiet. We have clearly marked this as another portion of the service, and age-old words of greeting are spoken in the *salutation* and *Sursum Corda*.

We Pray the Prayers of the People ⑯

Deacon: Let's join together in prayer, either out loud or quietly.

Leader: Let us take a moment to tell God "thank you" for all the good things that happen in our lives. Are there any special things we are grateful for? *(Pause)*

Leader: We say, "Thank you so much, Lord."
Assembly: Thank you so much, Lord.

Leader: Let us pray for those people or animals who are sick or who have died. *(Pause)*

Leader: We say, "God is with them."
Assembly: God is with them.

One of the most ancient acts of the Church is referred to as Intercessory Prayer. It is also one of the most holy. Holy means "set apart" or for very special use. Prayer is very, very special.

We ask God to help us and the people we care about. We give thanks for God's love for us and for those whom we love.

Please feel free to name things aloud or silently, any time during our prayer time.

We sing *(Please see songbook.)*

The Peace ⑰

The Announcements

We shake hands with those around us and say "Peace" or "The Peace of the Lord be with you."

⑱ **The Preparation of the Table and the Presentation of the Offerings**

Member of the Assembly: A gift is something we give; it is also something we are. It is time to give gifts of love, gifts of bread, gifts of money.

We sing *(Please see songbook.) As we sing, the* ⑲ *Deacon (Helper), the Priest (Elder) and some of our young seekers prepare the table.*

The sound of the bell calls us to silent prayer. ⑳

21 The text for the *Sanctus* (or Holy, Holy, Holy) is made comprehensible for our young worshippers and their family as well as other members of the assembly.

22 A young person elevates the bread as the Presider says the words of institution over the bread. In this same way, a young believer elevates the chalice and the cruet of wine as they are being blessed. At the *Epiclesis*, all hands in the room (not just the priest's) are laying hands of blessing on all the elements. We also invite the assembly to make a sign of the cross on themselves during the calling of the Holy Spirit to bless us.

The Holy Eucharist:

The Great Thanksgiving

Presider: The Lord is with you.
Assembly: The Lord is also with you.

Presider: Lift up your hearts.
Assembly: We lift them to the Lord.

Presider: Let us give thanks to the Lord our God.
Assembly: It is right to give God thanks and praise.

Presider: We praise you and we bless you, holy and gracious God, source of wisdom, light and hope.

We sing

Lord, You Are Holy (Sanctus)

Lord you are ho - ly. You are a God of power. You

glo - ry is ev - ry - where. Ho - san - na!

Presider: On the night he was handed over to suffering and death, Jesus gathered his friends, he took the bread, blessed and broke it and gave it to his friends and said,
Assembly: "This is my body. Whenever you eat this do this in remembrance of me."

Presider: Then Jesus took the cup filled with wine, raised it up and gave thanks for it, shared it with his friends and said,
Assembly: "This is my blood. Whenever you drink this, do this in remembrance of me."

Presider: We offer you these gifts,
Assembly: Jesus, the bread of life. Jesus, the cup of salvation.

Presider: Jesus Christ has died.
Assembly: Jesus Christ has died.
Presider: Jesus Christ has risen.
 Presider: Jesus Christ will come again.
Assembly: Jesus Christ will come again.

The Story of Jesus' meal with his friends.

Eucharist means "giving thanks" and here we give thanks for all the gifts God has given to us. We give some of our money to help the church do God's work. When we do this, we are saying that we do try to understand that all we have comes as a gift from God, including our money.

We join with the priest in blessing this meal. Feel free to join in the movements of the priest.

We say the bold words together.

In this prayer, we especially remember that God became human in Jesus, so that he could share our joys and sorrows with us. Jesus showed us by his life and teaching how God wants human life to be.

(23) Here we are in transition to sing a mighty, great *Amen*! And what an *Amen* it is! The assembly is on his or her feet singing and swaying and singing. We do it three times and each time it gets louder!

(24) In time, every member of the congregation largely understands the rise and fall of energy, movement, and volume enough that it is generally simple to go to a state of quiet during the Lord's Prayer. Various postures of prayer are encouraged and evidenced around the room. Some have palms up or folded or in an *orans* (palms open and raised up) posture. The ability to move from the energetic *Amen* to the quiet praying of the Lord's Prayer has grown to be one of the most profound moments in the service.

(25) As the bread is broken by the children and adults and put into bowls for the distribution, a longish song is sung many times. This gives time to prepare stations for Eucharist, fill more chalices, and place the young people. We generally have two communion stations (two breads and two wines), left and right of the table. We try to give chalices to older kids and they typically use the words, "The Blood of Christ." The bread is distributed, with the words, "The Body of Christ" by children who are only three years old! It is quite common to have a parent or adult helping with the bread as well as with the wine. When all is prepared, the Presider welcomes everyone to communion and says "The gifts of God for the People of God."

(26) During the distribution of communion, members of the assembly often go to an *ikonistasis* (icon stations) or side Lady Chapel to light candles for intercessions. There are stations of sand at a child's height as well as at adult height to light a candle and say a prayer. Singing of various songs continues throughout this time.

Presider: Send your Holy Spirit upon us and upon these gifts.

Assembly: Let them be for us the Body and Blood of your Son.

Presider: And grant that we who eat this bread and drink this cup may be filled with your life and goodness.

We sing

A - men (clap, clap) A - men (clap, clap) A - men, a-men, a - men!

© 2014 Dennis E. Northway. All rights reserved. Used with permission.

This part of the prayer is called the **Epiclesis**, which means the summoning (calling) of the Holy Spirit. The Church everywhere includes this in the Eucharistic Prayer. Please join in putting your arms out towards the bread and the wine.

This is known as the "Great Amen." **Amen** means "yes" or "so be it!" or "yes, I agree God!"

The Lord's Prayer

Presider: As our Savior Jesus Christ has taught us we now pray.

Assembly: Our Father in heaven, hallowed be your Name, your kingdom come, your will be done, on earth as it is in heaven. Give us today our daily bread. Forgive us our sins as we forgive those who sin against us. Save us from the time of trial; and deliver us from evil. For the kingdom, the power and the glory are yours, now and forever. Amen.

The Breaking of the Bread

We sing *(Please see songbook.)*

This bread is broken for us, we sing and we share communion with one another. We give the bread and say, "The Body of Christ (the Bread of Heaven)." We give the wine and say, "The Blood of Christ (the Cup of Salvation)."

(27) We have moved to occasionally have words that will "grow" with a child such as the words in this blessing. Though these words may be developmentally above the understanding of a three-year-old congregant, the words spoken by the priest will entice the child to curiosity. By this we simply mean, we know that we use words that a child might not quite understand yet. As they age, their language skills will change and so will their understanding of the many terms that are used in liturgies.

(28) The deacon or member of the assembly sends the assembly forth into the world. Children and adults depart for Christian Formation programs or social time.

(29) Again, a reminder of hospitality and how to be in touch with us.

A Final Prayer and A Blessing ㉗

Member of the Assembly or Presider: God we thank you for feeding us with this spiritual food and for your promise that we are children of God and saved by Jesus.
Assembly: Amen!

Presider: May the blessing of the God of Abraham and Sarah, and of Jesus Christ our Good Shepherd, born of our sister Mary, and of the Holy Spirit, who broods over the world as a mother hen over her chicks, be upon you and remain with you always.
Assembly: Amen!

The Priest offers God's blessings, God's divine protection, and God's thanks for the Assembly gathered.

Sending Us Into the World ㉘

Deacon: Go in peace, to love and serve the Lord. Alleluia, Alleluia!
Assembly: Thanks be to God! Alleluia, Alleluia!

The Deacon (Helper) dismisses the Assembly.

For more information about Grace Church, please be sure to sign the book at the entrance to the church, or fill out a pew card.

Also, for updated weekly emails from Grace, be sure to sign up on our website: www.GraceOakPark.org

Chapter 7:

The Liturgies

Make a joyful noise to the Lord, all the earth.
Worship the Lord with gladness;
come into his presence with singing.
Know that the Lord is God.
It is he that made us, and we are his;
we are his people, and the sheep of his pasture.
Enter his gates with thanksgiving,
and his courts with praise.
give thanks to him, bless his name.
For the Lord is good;
his steadfast love endures forever,
and his faithfulness to all generations.

(Psalm 100)

LITURGY IS THE WORK OF THE PEOPLE. ON THE FOLLOWING pages you will find The Rite Place liturgies for the various church seasons, plus a service of Holy Baptism and a Celebration of a Life. Yes, we have done a service for the Burial of the Dead at The Rite Place. We respect the dignity of children and their need to be part of all of life's celebrations, happy and sad.

Many people have contributed to the creation of these liturgies over the years as we have learned what resonates with children and families in worship, making adjustments and changes until it felt right. Our liturgies are joyful and prayerful. They invite movement and participation from everyone. We hope you will try them in your congregation and begin to develop similar liturgies that can truly be the work of your people. (Go to *www.churchpublishing.org/riteplace* to download a template to create your own liturgies.) Remember, when you speak directly to children, everyone listens.

The Rite Place
Advent

Welcome!

This liturgy is specifically designed for children and all in their households. Children (and adults) are active participants in an informal and relaxed setting wherein children are celebrated just as they are.

We are a church who firmly believes that all of God's children are welcome at the table of God. The liturgy is at the heart of all we do. From the full services on Sundays, to weekdays and the great feasts and seasons in the church year, we reach deeply into the riches of our Anglican tradition, building on it to explore new ways to give glory to God in our prayer, preaching and music.

We, like many others, find that when you speak directly to children, everyone listens. In this service, the teaching, the songs and the prayers will be aimed at the hearts and minds of our youngest worshippers, and all will learn something each week about the God who loves us.

We pray that this experience will be a wonderful way to connect adults with young children, and young children with adults. We strive to build a community where all feel a sense of hope and compassion from a church that welcomes all of God's children.

Advent

Advent is the Church's season of active expectation. Liturgy can be defined as the 'work of the people' [from the Greek *ergon* (work) + *laos* (people)] as we gather to pray and praise.   In Advent, as in all the seasons of the church, we wish to express importance of the participation of everyone in worship. So we invite you and your family to bring all of your senses to the experience: look around and notice how our church, a sacred space, is structured and decorated, how the lighting grows as we advance ever closer to Christmas. Listen to the prayers and the songs. Sniff the air for unmistakable signs of the season. Lift your own voice—and encourage others around you to do the same—as we pray and sing together to remind ourselves and others that God is with us still (the meaning of *Emmanuel)*. And then wind your way back out into the world which God continues to love, and spread the word as you do the work God has called you to do every day of the week.

Making and using Advent wreaths is an ancient custom of the church. While there are many different versions of what the wreaths themselves mean or symbolize, most of us can get to the center of the meaning by knowing that the wreath is a way to mark the journey looking back at and towards the birth of little baby Jesus. We have adapted the model of having the four candles (for each week of Advent) in a circle close together, to instead, have four candles surrounded with greens in the midst of our congregation. They invite us, you and me, to be the wreath as we worship and walk up to communion. They enfold us and include us in the weekly journey of reflecting on the birth of Christ.

Watch for these symbols and meanings:

| Procession | Shofar | Music | Crosses | Bell |
| Prayer | Bible Readings | Communion | Welcome & Dismissal | Holy Spirit |

**We gather with our questions
as spiritual seekers on a journey.**

We gather to find God.

A Gathering Time

 Welcome

We gather in the name of the God three-in-one or the Triune God, at the entrance to the church. We say hello to God and one another. We take time to see and welcome our neighbor.

We prepare.

 Sounding of the Shofar

Israel used the ram's horn, called a shofar, to call together the people of God.

Member or Presider of the Assembly: Welcome in the name of God: Creator, Shepherd, and Wind.
Assembly: Amen.

 Opening Song

We sing a gathering song and process down the center aisle.

The Procession

Please feel free to carry an instrument, streamer, cross, or candle as we walk down the aisle. Place these objects in the wicker baskets when we approach and surround the table.

 We Begin to Pray

The Collect of the Day

Member or Presider of the Assembly: God is with you.
Assembly: God is also with you.

This prayer is called the Collect. The Leader or Priest "collects" or "gathers" the themes of the lesson, the church season, and the congregation into one prayer.

Member or Presider of the Assembly: Let us pray.

Dear God, we want to make a smooth path for you.
Be with us as we wait for Jesus. **Amen.**

The Word of God: God Speaks.

We Listen and Respond.

We sing

(The song will be announced.)

A Story from the Hebrew Bible (Old Testament) or New Testament

Reader: Hear what the Spirit is saying to God's people.
Assembly: Thanks be to God.

or

Deacon: The Good News about Jesus as told by

_____.

Gospel Refrain
Assembly:

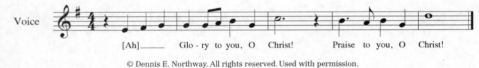

Voice   [Ah]_____ Glo - ry to you, O Christ!   Praise to you, O Christ!

© Dennis E. Northway. All rights reserved. Used with permission.

After the Gospel, the Deacon says: This is the Good News of the Good Shepherd.

We sing the *Gospel Refrain* again.

Homily

The sound of the bell calls us to a moment of silence.

The Old Testament is also known as the Hebrew Bible, and contains the books that were written before Jesus was born. The New Testament contains the Gospels and Epistles (letters) and the Book of Acts written by a person who knew about Jesus.

The Deacon (or someone else) tells us the story found in the Gospel appointed for this Sunday of the Church Year. This reading is always from one of four books, Matthew, Mark, Luke or John found in the Bible.

We talk about the scripture reading and what it means for us and how we live our lives.

We Pray the Prayers of the People

Deacon: It is time to pray to God. We join together to name our concerns or joys aloud or in quiet prayer.

Leader: Sometimes things go wrong, or we do wrong. We are sorry for them. Are there things for which we are sorry? *(Pause)*

Leader: We say, "Lord, we are sorry."
Assembly: Lord, we are sorry.

Leader: Let us take a moment to tell God "thank you" for all the just plain good things that happen in our lives. Are there any special things we are grateful for? *(Pause)*

Leader: We say, "Thank you so much, Lord."
Assembly: Thank you so much, Lord.

Leader: Let us pray for those people or animals who have died. *(Pause)*

Leader: We say, "God is with them."
Assembly: God is with them.

Leader: Sometimes we know people who are sick or we are worried about something in our lives. Are there any special needs, concerns or worries we should tell God about? *(Pause)*

Leader: We say, "Help us always, Lord."
Assembly: Help us always, Lord.

We sing *(Please see songbook.)*

The Peace

The Announcements

The Preparation of the Table and the Presentation of the Offerings

Member of the Assembly: A gift is something we give; it is also something we are. It is time to give gifts of love, gifts of bread, gifts of money.

One of the most ancient acts of the Church is referred to as Intercessory Prayer. It is also one of the most holy. Holy means "set apart" or for very special use. Prayer is very, very special.

We ask God to help us and the people we care about. We give thanks for God's love for us and for those whom we love.

Please feel free to name things aloud or silently, any time during our prayer time.

We shake hands with those around us and say "Peace" or "The Peace of the Lord be with you."

We sing *(Please see songbook.) As we sing, the Deacon (Helper), the Priest (Elder) and some of our young seekers prepare the table.*

 The sound of the bell calls us to silent prayer.

The Holy Eucharist:

 ### The Great Thanksgiving

Presider: The Lord is with you.
Assembly: The Lord is also with you.

Presider: Lift up your hearts.
Assembly: We lift them to the Lord.

Presider: Let us give thanks to the Lord our God.
Assembly: It is right to give God thanks and praise.

Presider: We praise you and we bless you, holy and gracious God, source of wisdom, light and hope.

 We sing

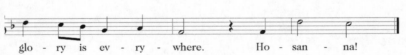

Lord, You Are Holy (Sanctus)

Lord you are ho - ly. You are a God of power. You glo - ry is ev - ry - where. Ho - san - na!

© 2009 Dennis E. Northway. All rights reserved. Used with permission.

 Presider: On the night he was handed over to suffering and death, Jesus gathered his friends, he took the bread, blessed and broke it and gave it to his friends and said,
Assembly: "This is my body. Whenever you eat this do this in remembrance of me."

Presider: Then Jesus took the cup filled with wine, raised it up and gave thanks for it, shared it with his friends and said,
Assembly: "This is my blood. Whenever you drink this, do this in remembrance of me."

The Story of Jesus' meal with his friends.

Eucharist means "giving thanks" and here we give thanks for all the gifts God has given to us. We give some of our money to help the church do God's work. When we do this, we are saying that we do try to understand that all we have comes as a gift from God, including our money.

We join with the priest in blessing this meal. Feel free to join in the movements of the priest.

We say the bold words together.

In this prayer, we especially remember that God became human in Jesus, so that he could share our joys and sorrows with us. Jesus showed us by his life and teaching how God wants human life to be.

Presider: We offer you these gifts,
Assembly: Jesus, the bread of life. Jesus, the cup of salvation.

Presider: Jesus Christ has died.
Assembly: Jesus Christ has died.
Presider: Jesus Christ has risen.
Assembly: Jesus Christ has risen.
Presider: Jesus Christ will come again.
Assembly: Jesus Christ will come again.

Presider: Send your Holy Spirit upon us and upon these gifts.
Assembly: Let them be for us the Body and Blood of your Son.

Presider: And grant that we who eat this bread and drink this cup may be filled with your life and goodness.

This part of the prayer is called the *Epiclesis*, which means the summoning (calling) of the Holy Spirit. The Church everywhere includes this in the Eucharistic Prayer. Please join in putting your arms out towards the bread and the wine.

We sing

This is known as the "Great Amen." *Amen* means "yes" or "so be it!" or "yes, I agree God!"

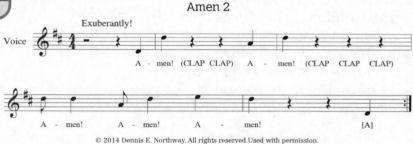

Amen 2

Voice — Exuberantly!

A - men! (CLAP CLAP) A - men! (CLAP CLAP CLAP)

A - men! A - men! A - men! [A]

The Lord's Prayer

Presider: As our Savior Jesus Christ has taught us we now pray.
Assembly: Our Father in heaven, hallowed be your Name, your kingdom come, your will be done, on earth as it is in heaven. Give us today our daily bread. Forgive us our sins as we forgive those who sin against us. Save us from the time of trial; and deliver us from evil. For the kingdom, the power and the glory are yours, now and forever. Amen.

The Breaking of the Bread

This bread is broken for us, we sing and we share communion with one another. We give the bread and say, "The Body of Christ (the Bread of Heaven)." We give the wine and say, "The Blood of Christ (the Cup of Salvation)."

 We sing *(Please see songbook.)*

A Final Prayer and A Blessing

 Member of the Assembly or Presider: God, we thank you for feeding us with this spiritual food, and for your promise that we are children of God and saved by Jesus. We have gathered and sung; we have feasted and prayed. Be with us now as we go away from this place, out into the world to live as Jesus would have us live.

Assembly: Amen!

Presider: In this holy season of wonder and waiting, afford our hearts the possibility of mystical ecstasy coupled with transcendent calm. Bless our souls with peace and intentionality, with joy, and surprise. Be Lord, in our hearts, in our deeds, in our minds. Smile upon your people who hope only in you. And the blessing of God almighty, creator, redeemer, and sanctifier be with you this day and evermore.

Assembly: Amen!

The Priest offers God's blessings, God's divine protection, and God's thanks for the Assembly gathered.

Sending Us Into the World

 Deacon: Go in peace, to love and serve the Lord.
Assembly: Thanks be to God!

The Deacon (Helper) dismisses the Assembly.

The Rite Place

Christmas

Welcome!

This liturgy is specifically designed for children and all in their households. Children (and adults) are active participants in an informal and relaxed setting wherein children are celebrated just as they are.

We are a church who firmly believes that all of God's children are welcome at the table of God. The liturgy is at the heart of all we do. From the full services on Sundays, to weekdays and the great feasts and seasons in the church year, we reach deeply into the riches of our Anglican tradition, building on it to explore new ways to give glory to God in our prayer, preaching and music.

We, like many others, find that when you speak directly to children, everyone listens. In this service, the teaching, the songs and the prayers will be aimed at the hearts and minds of our youngest worshippers, and all will learn something each week about the God who loves us.

We pray that this experience will be a wonderful way to connect adults with young children, and young children with adults. We strive to build a community where all feel a sense of hope and compassion from a church that welcomes all of God's children.

Christmas

We all love the holidays, especially Christmas! Holiday literally comes from "holy day" in earlier English use. What does it specifically mean to be holy? From the prophet Isaiah, we hear that special things in the Temple were "Kadosh" or "set apart" for specific use in the surrounds and rituals of the Temple. To be holy is literally to be set apart for special purposes. When we keep a holiday, we set it aside and make it holy. When Jesus was born to Mary and Joseph, a long time ago, the world was radically changed. During the season of Christmas we celebrate Jesus as *Emmanuel*, God with us. Jesus taught us as he lived and ministered, to be love to people who have no love, to help the poor and the disaffected. The birth of Jesus reminds us that, as Christ came to Earth to help and save us, we should also, after gathering to thank God for all God's gifts, go out into the world to be Christ to a needy and broken world. To do that is to be set apart, or to be given a holy purpose. We celebrate the birth of Jesus and bask in the glow of a truly holy day!

Watch for these symbols and meanings:

| Procession | Shofar | Music | Crosses | Bell |

| Prayer | Bible Readings | Communion | Welcome & Dismissal | Holy Spirit |

**We gather with our questions
as spiritual seekers on a journey.**

We gather to find God.

A Gathering Time

Welcome

We gather in the name of the God three-in-one or the Triune God, at the entrance to the church. We say hello to God and one another. We take time to see and welcome our neighbor.

We prepare.

Sounding of the Shofar

Israel used the ram's horn, called a shofar, to call together the people of God.

Member or Presider of the Assembly: Welcome in the name of God: Creator, Shepherd, and Wind.
Assembly: Amen.

Opening Song

We sing a gathering song and process down the center aisle.

The Procession

Please feel free to carry an instrument, streamer, cross, or candle as we walk down the aisle. Place these objects in the wicker baskets when we approach and surround the table.

We Begin to Pray

The Collect of the Day

Member or Presider of the Assembly: God is with you.
Assembly: God is also with you.

This prayer is called the Collect. The Leader or Priest "collects" or "gathers" the themes of the lesson, the church season, and the congregation into one prayer.

Member or Presider of the Assembly: Let us pray.

Thank you, God, for all the fun of Christmas and especially for sending the baby Jesus to live with us.
Amen.

The Word of God: God Speaks.

We Listen and Respond.

 We sing

(The song will be announced.)

 A Story from the Hebrew Bible (Old Testament) or New Testament

Reader: Hear what the Spirit is saying to God's people.
Assembly: Thanks be to God.

or

Deacon: The Good News about Jesus as told by
_____.

> The Old Testament is also known as the Hebrew Bible, and contains the books that were written before Jesus was born. The New Testament contains the Gospels and Epistles (letters) and the Book of Acts written by a person who knew about Jesus.

Gospel Refrain
Assembly:

[Ah]_____ Glo - ry to you, O Christ! Praise to you, O Christ!

> The Deacon (or someone else) tells us the story found in the Gospel appointed for this Sunday of the Church Year. This reading is always from one of four books, Matthew, Mark, Luke or John found in the Bible.

After the Gospel, the Deacon says: This is the Good News of the Good Shepherd.

 We sing the *Gospel Refrain* again.

 Homily

> We talk about the scripture reading and what it means for us and how we live our lives.

 The sound of the bell calls us to a moment of silence.

We Pray the Prayers of the People

One of the most ancient acts of the Church is referred to as Intercessory Prayer. It is also one of the most holy. Holy means "set apart" or for very special use. Prayer is very, very special.

We ask God to help us and the people we care about. We give thanks for God's love for us and for those whom we love.

Please feel free to name things aloud or silently, any time during our prayer time.

Deacon: It is time to pray to God. We join together to name our concerns or joys aloud or in quiet prayer.

Leader: Sometimes things go wrong, or we do wrong. We are sorry for them. Are there things for which we are sorry? *(Pause)*

Leader: We say, "Lord, we are sorry."
Assembly: Lord, we are sorry.

Leader: Let us take a moment to tell God "thank you" for all the just plain good things that happen in our lives. Are there any special things we are grateful for? *(Pause)*

Leader: We say, "Thank you so much, Lord."
Assembly: Thank you so much, Lord.

Leader: Let us pray for those people or animals who have died. *(Pause)*

Leader: We say, "God is with them."
Assembly: God is with them.

Leader: Sometimes we know people who are sick or we are worried about something in our lives. Are there any special needs, concerns or worries we should tell God about? *(Pause)*

Leader: We say, "Help us always, Lord."
Assembly: Help us always, Lord.

We sing *(Please see songbook.)*

The Peace

The Announcements

We shake hands with those around us and say "Peace" or "The Peace of the Lord be with you."

The Preparation of the Table and the Presentation of the Offerings

Member of the Assembly: A gift is something we give; it is also something we are. It is time to give gifts of love, gifts of bread, gifts of money.

We sing *(Please see songbook.) As we sing, the Deacon (Helper), the Priest (Elder) and some of our young seekers prepare the table.*

 The sound of the bell calls us to silent prayer.

The Holy Eucharist:

 The Great Thanksgiving

Presider: The Lord is with you.
Assembly: The Lord is also with you.

Presider: Lift up your hearts.
Assembly: We lift them to the Lord.

Presider: Let us give thanks to the Lord our God.
Assembly: It is right to give God thanks and praise.

Presider: We praise you and we bless you, holy and gracious God, source of wisdom, light and hope.

 We sing

Lord, You Are Holy (Sanctus)

Lord you are ho-ly. You are a God of power. You glo-ry is ev-ry-where. Ho-san-na!

© 2009 Dennis E. Northway. All rights reserved. Used with permission.

 Presider: On the night he was handed over to suffering and death, Jesus gathered his friends, he took the bread, blessed and broke it and gave it to his friends and said,
Assembly: "This is my body. Whenever you eat this do this in remembrance of me."

Presider: Then Jesus took the cup filled with wine, raised it up and gave thanks for it, shared it with his friends and said,

The Story of Jesus' meal with his friends.

Eucharist means "giving thanks" and here we give thanks for all the gifts God has given to us. We give some of our money to help the church do God's work. When we do this, we are saying that we do try to understand that all we have comes as a gift from God, including our money.

We join with the priest in blessing this meal. Feel free to join in the movements of the priest.

We say the bold words together.

In this prayer, we especially remember that God became human in Jesus, so that he could share our joys and sorrows with us. Jesus showed us by his life and teaching how God wants human life to be.

Assembly: "This is my blood. Whenever you drink this, do this in remembrance of me."

Presider: We offer you these gifts,

Assembly: Jesus, the bread of life. Jesus, the cup of salvation.

Presider: Jesus Christ has died.

Assembly: Jesus Christ has died.

Presider: Jesus Christ has risen.

Assembly: Jesus Christ has risen.

Presider: Jesus Christ will come again.

Assembly: Jesus Christ will come again.

Presider: Send your Holy Spirit upon us and upon these gifts.

Assembly: Let them be for us the Body and Blood of your Son.

Presider: And grant that we who eat this bread and drink this cup may be filled with your life and goodness.

This part of the prayer is called the *Epiclesis*, which means the summoning (calling) of the Holy Spirit. The Church everywhere includes this in the Eucharistic Prayer. Please join in putting your arms out towards the bread and the wine.

We sing

This is known as the "Great Amen." *Amen* means "yes" or "so be it!" or "yes, I agree God!"

The Lord's Prayer

Presider: As our Savior Jesus Christ has taught us we now pray.

Assembly: Our Father in heaven, hallowed be your Name, your kingdom come, your will be done, on earth as it is in heaven. Give us today our daily bread. Forgive us our sins as we forgive those who sin against us. Save us from the time of trial; and deliver us from evil. For the kingdom, the power and the glory are yours, now and forever. Amen.

The Breaking of the Bread

This bread is broken for us, we sing and we share communion with one another. We give the bread and say, "The Body of Christ (the Bread of Heaven)." We give the wine and say, "The Blood of Christ (the Cup of Salvation)."

 We sing *(Please see songbook.)*

A Final Prayer and A Blessing

 Member of the Assembly or Presider: God we thank you for feeding us with this spiritual food and for your promise that we are children of God and saved by Jesus.
Assembly: Amen!
Presider: May the blessing of the God of Abraham and Sarah, and of Jesus Christ our Good Shepherd, born of our sister Mary, and of the Holy Spirit, who broods over the world as a mother hen over her chicks, be upon you and remain with you always.
Assembly: Amen!

The Priest offers God's blessings, God's divine protection, and God's thanks for the Assembly gathered.

Sending Us Into the World

 Deacon: Go in peace, to love and serve the Lord.
Assembly: Thanks be to God!

The Deacon (Helper) dismisses the Assembly.

The Rite Place

Epiphany

Welcome!

This liturgy is specifically designed for children and all in their households. Children (and adults) are active participants in an informal and relaxed setting wherein children are celebrated just as they are.

We are a church who firmly believes that all of God's children are welcome at the table of God. The liturgy is at the heart of all we do. From the full services on Sundays, to weekdays and the great feasts and seasons in the church year, we reach deeply into the riches of our Anglican tradition, building on it to explore new ways to give glory to God in our prayer, preaching and music.

We, like many others, find that when you speak directly to children, everyone listens. In this service, the teaching, the songs and the prayers will be aimed at the hearts and minds of our youngest worshippers, and all will learn something each week about the God who loves us.

We pray that this experience will be a wonderful way to connect adults with young children, and young children with adults. We strive to build a community where all feel a sense of hope and compassion from a church that welcomes all of God's children.

Epiphany

"And lo, they followed the star . . ." The magi, we are told, followed the star to Bethlehem to worship Jesus, and when they got there, they offered their gifts. Epiphany is a time in the church year to trace the life, work, teaching, and miracles of Jesus as we gather and tell our story on Sunday morning. We begin with the Feast of Epiphany and the coming of the magi—foreigners/people from another land. However, we also expand our theme to the Light of Christ coming to a needy and broken world. During this season of Epiphany (Epiphany literally means "to be revealed"), we, as a community, share our story of Jesus, say thanks to God for life and health and family and friends; we also say we are sorry and ask forgiveness. We share Eucharist, or communion, and then, just like the magi, we go and offer our gifts to a broken and sinful world. We go to be Light in the darkness! Halleluia!

Watch for these symbols and meanings:

| Procession | Shofar | Music | Crosses | Bell |
| Prayer | Bible Readings | Communion | Welcome & Dismissal | Holy Spirit |

**We gather with our questions
as spiritual seekers on a journey.**

We gather to find God.

A Gathering Time

Welcome

We gather in the name of the God three-in-one or the Triune God, at the entrance to the church. We say hello to God and one another. We take time to see and welcome our neighbor.

We prepare.

Sounding of the Shofar

Israel used the ram's horn, called a shofar, to call together the people of God.

Member or Presider of the Assembly: Welcome in the name of God: Creator, Shepherd, and Wind.
Assembly: Amen.

Opening Song

We sing a gathering song and process down the center aisle.

The Procession

Please feel free to carry an instrument, streamer, cross, or candle as we walk down the aisle. Place these objects in the wicker baskets when we approach and surround the table.

We Begin to Pray

The Collect of the Day

Member or Presider of the Assembly: God is with you.
Assembly: God is also with you.

Member or Presider of the Assembly: Let us pray.

Thank you, God, for sending Jesus to be the light of the world. Help us to also show your love to the world. **Amen**.

This prayer is called the Collect. The Leader or Priest "collects" or "gathers" the themes of the lesson, the church season, and the congregation into one prayer.

The Word of God: God Speaks.

We Listen and Respond.

We sing

(The song will be announced.)

A Story from the Hebrew Bible (Old Testament) or New Testament

Reader: Hear what the Spirit is saying to God's people.
Assembly: Thanks be to God.

or

Deacon: The Good News about Jesus as told by
_____.

Gospel Refrain
Assembly:

Voice

[Ah]_____ Glo - ry to you, O Christ! Praise to you, O Christ!

© Dennis E. Northway. All rights reserved. Used with permission.

After the Gospel, the Deacon says: This is the Good News of the Good Shepherd.

We sing the *Gospel Refrain* again.

Homily

The sound of the bell calls us to a moment of silence.

The Old Testament is also known as the Hebrew Bible, and contains the books that were written before Jesus was born. The New Testament contains the Gospels and Epistles (letters) and the Book of Acts written by a person who knew about Jesus.

The Deacon (or someone else) tells us the story found in the Gospel appointed for this Sunday of the Church Year. This reading is always from one of four books, Matthew, Mark, Luke or John found in the Bible.

We talk about the scripture reading and what it means for us and how we live our lives.

We Pray the Prayers of the People

Deacon: It is time to pray to God. We join together to name our concerns or joys aloud or in quiet prayer.

Leader: Sometimes things go wrong, or we do wrong. We are sorry for them. Are there things for which we are sorry? *(Pause)*

Leader: We say, "Lord, we are sorry."
Assembly: Lord, we are sorry.

Leader: Let us take a moment to tell God "thank you" for all the just plain good things that happen in our lives. Are there any special things we are grateful for? *(Pause)*

Leader: We say, "Thank you so much, Lord."
Assembly: Thank you so much, Lord.

Leader: Let us pray for those people or animals who have died. *(Pause)*

Leader: We say, "God is with them."
Assembly: God is with them.

Leader: Sometimes we know people who are sick or we are worried about something in our lives. Are there any special needs, concerns or worries we should tell God about? *(Pause)*

Leader: We say, "Help us always, Lord."
Assembly: Help us always, Lord.

One of the most ancient acts of the Church is referred to as Intercessory Prayer. It is also one of the most holy. Holy means "set apart" or for very special use. Prayer is very, very special.

We ask God to help us and the people we care about. We give thanks for God's love for us and for those whom we love.

Please feel free to name things aloud or silently, any time during our prayer time.

We sing *(Please see songbook.)*

The Peace

The Announcements

The Preparation of the Table and the Presentation of the Offerings

Member of the Assembly: A gift is something we give; it is also something we are. It is time to give gifts of love, gifts of bread, gifts of money.

We shake hands with those around us and say "Peace" or "The Peace of the Lord be with you."

We sing *(Please see songbook.) As we sing, the Deacon (Helper), the Priest (Elder) and some of our young seekers prepare the table.*

 The sound of the bell calls us to silent prayer.

The Holy Eucharist:

 The Great Thanksgiving

Presider: The Lord is with you.
Assembly: The Lord is also with you.

Presider: Lift up your hearts.
Assembly: We lift them to the Lord.

Presider: Let us give thanks to the Lord our God.
Assembly: It is right to give God thanks and praise.

Presider: We praise you and we bless you, holy and gracious God, source of wisdom, light and hope.

 We sing

The Story of Jesus' meal with his friends.

Eucharist means "giving thanks" and here we give thanks for all the gifts God has given to us. We give some of our money to help the church do God's work. When we do this, we are saying that we do try to understand that all we have comes as a gift from God, including our money.

Lord, You Are Holy (Sanctus)

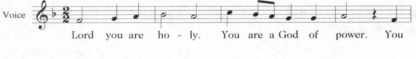

Lord you are ho-ly. You are a God of power. You

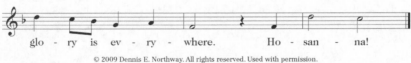

glo-ry is ev-ry-where. Ho-san-na!

© 2009 Dennis E. Northway. All rights reserved. Used with permission.

 Presider: On the night he was handed over to suffering and death, Jesus gathered his friends, he took the bread, blessed and broke it and gave it to his friends and said,
Assembly: "This is my body. Whenever you eat this do this in remembrance of me."

Presider: Then Jesus took the cup filled with wine, raised it up and gave thanks for it, shared it with his friends and said,
Assembly: "This is my blood. Whenever you drink this, do this in remembrance of me."

We join with the priest in blessing this meal. Feel free to join in the movements of the priest.

We say the bold words together.

In this prayer, we especially remember that God became human in Jesus, so that he could share our joys and sorrows with us. Jesus showed us by his life and teaching how God wants human life to be.

Presider: We offer you these gifts,
Assembly: Jesus, the bread of life. Jesus, the cup of salvation.

Presider: Jesus Christ has died.
Assembly: Jesus Christ has died.
Presider: Jesus Christ has risen.
Assembly: Jesus Christ has risen.
Presider: Jesus Christ will come again.
Assembly: Jesus Christ will come again.

Presider: Send your Holy Spirit upon us and upon these gifts.
Assembly: Let them be for us the Body and Blood of your Son.

Presider: And grant that we who eat this bread and drink this cup may be filled with your life and goodness.

We sing

This part of the prayer is called the *Epiclesis*, which means the summoning (calling) of the Holy Spirit. The Church everywhere includes this in the Eucharistic Prayer. Please join in putting your arms out towards the bread and the wine.

This is known as the "Great Amen." *Amen* means "yes" or "so be it!" or "yes, I agree God!"

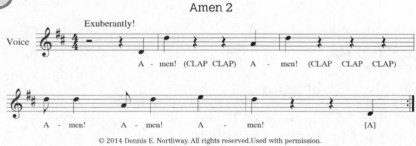

Amen 2

A - men! (CLAP CLAP) A - men! (CLAP CLAP CLAP)

A - men! A - men! A - men! [A]

The Lord's Prayer

Presider: As our Savior Jesus Christ has taught us we now pray.
Assembly: Our Father in heaven, hallowed be your Name, your kingdom come, your will be done, on earth as it is in heaven. Give us today our daily bread. Forgive us our sins as we forgive those who sin against us. Save us from the time of trial; and deliver us from evil. For the kingdom, the power and the glory are yours, now and forever. Amen.

The Breaking of the Bread

This bread is broken for us, we sing and we share communion with one another. We give the bread and say, "The Body of Christ (the Bread of Heaven)." We give the wine and say, "The Blood of Christ (the Cup of Salvation)."

 We sing *(Please see songbook.)*

A Final Prayer and A Blessing

 Member of the Assembly or Presider: God we thank you for feeding us with this spiritual food and for your promise that we are children of God and saved by Jesus.
Assembly: Amen!

Presider: May the blessing of the God of Abraham and Sarah, and of Jesus Christ our Good Shepherd, born of our sister Mary, and of the Holy Spirit, who broods over the world as a mother hen over her chicks, be upon you and remain with you always.
Assembly: Amen!

The Priest offers God's blessings, God's divine protection, and God's thanks for the Assembly gathered.

Sending Us Into the World

 Assembly: Send us forth with a blessing.

Presider: May the Almighty God who is Lord in our hearts, in our deeds and in our minds, smile upon you. And the blessing of God Almighty, Creator, Shepherd, and Wind be upon you this day and evermore.
Assembly: Amen.

Deacon: Go in peace, to love and serve the Lord.
Assembly: Thanks be to God!

The Deacon (Helper) dismisses the Assembly.

The Rite Place

Lent

Welcome!

This liturgy is specifically designed for children and all in their households. Children (and adults) are active participants in an informal and relaxed setting wherein children are celebrated just as they are.

We are a church who firmly believes that all of God's children are welcome at the table of God. The liturgy is at the heart of all we do. From the full services on Sundays, to weekdays and the great feasts and seasons in the church year, we reach deeply into the riches of our Anglican tradition, building on it to explore new ways to give glory to God in our prayer, preaching and music.

We, like many others, find that when you speak directly to children, everyone listens. In this service, the teaching, the songs and the prayers will be aimed at the hearts and minds of our youngest worshippers, and all will learn something each week about the God who loves us.

We pray that this experience will be a wonderful way to connect adults with young children, and young children with adults. We strive to build a community where all feel a sense of hope and compassion from a church that welcomes all of God's children.

Lent

Lent is a border-walking time: death and life, glory and shame, sin and grace, temptation and repentance, all littering the Lenten landscape; all halting us in our liturgical tracks for a forty-day blink of the inner eye. There are many ways to observe Lent. Some make behavioral or culinary changes, some fast, some pray more, some create more space for quiet or introspection. There are many ways to observe a Holy Lent. There is no one right way.

In the earliest history of the Christian church, there was no Lent. Instead, the time leading up to Easter was a time of careful preparation by those who wanted to be baptized as Christians to learn about their faith and their new life in Christ. One way to walk through Lent could be as a reflection of, and about, our Baptismal Covenant. The promises you made, or were made on your behalf, are found in the *Book of Common Prayer*, pages 302-304.

Though the mystery of God is always very near us, Lent is one of those seasons when we are invited to carve for ourselves. Take a few moments to pay attention to that mystery of God, which is always hovering, finger-tip close, heart-chambered, nestled in ourselves and nestled in our neighbor, too. Ponder, what would this look like in your life this Lent? Lent is also a time for taking advantage of the gifts we are offered. We can seize the grace that is given us and use it to make a better world!

Take a moment and let the journey begin!

Watch for these symbols and meanings:

Procession   Shofar   Music   Crosses   Bell

Prayer   Bible Readings   Communion   Welcome & Dismissal   Holy Spirit

**We gather with our questions
as spiritual seekers on a journey.**

We gather to find God.

A Gathering Time

Welcome

We gather in the name of the God three-in-one or the Triune God, at the entrance to the church. We say hello to God and one another. We take time to see and welcome our neighbor.

We prepare.

Sounding of the Shofar

Israel used the ram's horn, called a shofar, to call together the people of God.

Member or Presider of the Assembly: Welcome. Bless be the God who forgives all our sins.
Assembly: God's mercy endures forever.

Opening Song

We sing a gathering song and process down the center aisle.

The Procession

Please feel free to carry an instrument, streamer, cross, or candle as we walk down the aisle. Place these objects in the wicker baskets when we approach and surround the table.

We Begin to Pray
The Collect of the Day

This prayer is called the Collect. The Leader or Priest "collects" or "gathers" the themes of the lesson, the church season, and the congregation into one prayer.

Member or Presider of the Assembly: God is with you.
Assembly: God is also with you.

Member or Presider of the Assembly: Let us pray.

Jesus, you are the way through the wilderness: show us your truth in which we walk, and by the gift of the Holy Spirit draw us to God. **Amen**.

The Word of God: God Speaks.

We Listen and Respond.

We sing

(The song will be announced.)

A Story from the Hebrew Bible (Old Testament) or New Testament

Reader: Hear what the Spirit is saying to God's people.
Assembly: Thanks be to God.

or

Deacon: The Good News about Jesus as told by _____.

Gospel Refrain
Assembly:

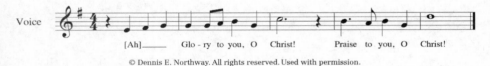

Voice

[Ah]_____ Glo - ry to you, O Christ! Praise to you, O Christ!

After the Gospel, the Deacon says: This is the Good News of the Good Shepherd.

The Old Testament is also known as the Hebrew Bible, and contains the books that were written before Jesus was born. The New Testament contains the Gospels and Epistles (letters) and the Book of Acts written by a person who knew about Jesus.

The Deacon (or someone else) tells us the story found in the Gospel appointed for this Sunday of the Church Year. This reading is always from one of four books, Matthew, Mark, Luke or John found in the Bible.

We sing the *Gospel Refrain* again.

Homily

We talk about the scripture reading and what it means for us and how we live our lives.

The sound of the bell calls us to a moment of silence.

We Pray the Prayers of the People

One of the most ancient acts of the Church is referred to as Intercessory Prayer. It is also one of the most holy. Holy means "set apart" or for very special use. Prayer is very, very special.

We ask God to help us and the people we care about. We give thanks for God's love for us and for those whom we love.

Please feel free to name things aloud or silently, any time during our prayer time.

Said or sung by a cantor or member of the Assembly: Dear God, thank you so, so much for our moms, dads, children, relatives, friends, and pets. *(Pause)*

Cantor: They make us happy, and we know they make you happy, so we sing: God we have made you glad. Bless us.

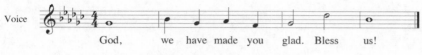

Cantor: Dear God, sometimes what we have done has made you sad *(Pause)*

Cantor: and we are sorry, so we sing: God we have made you sad. Bless us.
Assembly: God we have made you sad. Bless us.

Cantor: Dear God, sometimes people are mean, or bad or grumpy, or do not do the right things *(Pause)*

Cantor: and we are sorry, so we sing: God we have made you mad. Bless us.
Assembly: God we have made you mad. Bless us.

Cantor: Dear God, sometimes things go wrong, or there are problems at home, or school, or in the world. People get sick. People die. *(Pause)*

Cantor: So we sing: God, we with you are sad. Bless us.
Assembly: God, we with you are sad. Bless us.

Cantor: Dear God, we are in Lent, help this to be a special time in our life. Help us to pray to you all the time and help other people as well. We know this makes you glad, so we sing: God we have made you glad. Bless us.
Assembly: God we have made you glad. Bless us.

Confession

We tell God we are sorry.

Presider or Deacon: God of mercy
Assembly: God of mercy

Presider or Deacon: We are sorry
Assembly: We are sorry

Presider or Deacon: Truly sorry
Assembly: Truly sorry

Presider or Deacon: And we ask your forgiveness
Assembly: And we ask your forgiveness

Presider or Deacon: Help us walk in the way of your love
Assembly: Help us walk in the way of your love. Amen.

Absolution

We are forgiven.

 We sing *(Please see songbook.)*

The Peace

The Announcements

We shake hands with those around us and say "Peace" or "The Peace of the Lord be with you."

The Preparation of the Table and the Presentation of the Offerings

Member of the Assembly: A gift is something we give; it is also something we are. It is time to give gifts of love, gifts of bread, gifts of money.

 We sing *(Please see songbook.) As we sing, the Deacon (Helper), the Priest (Elder) and some of our young seekers prepare the table.*

 The sound of the bell calls us to silent prayer.

The Holy Eucharist:

The Story of Jesus' meal with his friends.

 The Great Thanksgiving

Eucharist means "giving thanks" and here we give thanks for all the gifts God has given to us. We give some of our money to help the church do God's work. When we do this, we are saying that we do try to understand that all we have comes as a gift from God, including our money.

Presider: The Lord is with you.
Assembly: The Lord is also with you.

Presider: Lift up your hearts.
Assembly: We lift them to the Lord.

Presider: Let us give thanks to the Lord our God.
Assembly: It is right to give God thanks and praise.

Presider: We praise you and we bless you, holy and gracious God, source of wisdom, light and hope.

We sing

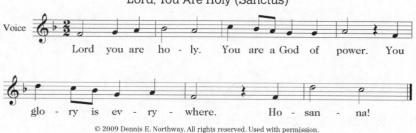

Lord, You Are Holy (Sanctus)

Voice
Lord you are ho - ly. You are a God of power. You glo - ry is ev - ry - where. Ho - san - na!

Presider: On the night he was handed over to suffering and death, Jesus gathered his friends, he took the bread, blessed and broke it and gave it to his friends and said,
Assembly: "This is my body. Whenever you eat this do this in remembrance of me."

Presider: Then Jesus took the cup filled with wine, raised it up and gave thanks for it, shared it with his friends and said,
Assembly: "This is my blood. Whenever you drink this, do this in remembrance of me."

Presider: We offer you these gifts,
Assembly: Jesus, the bread of life. Jesus, the cup of salvation.

Presider: Jesus Christ has died.
Assembly: Jesus Christ has died.
Presider: Jesus Christ has risen.
Assembly: Jesus Christ has risen.
Presider: Jesus Christ will come again.
Assembly: Jesus Christ will come again.

Presider: Send your Holy Spirit upon us and upon these gifts.
Assembly: Let them be for us the Body and Blood of your Son.

Presider: And grant that we who eat this bread and drink this cup may be filled with your life and goodness.

We join with the priest in blessing this meal. Feel free to join in the movements of the priest.

We say the bold words together.

In this prayer, we especially remember that God became human in Jesus, so that he could share our joys and sorrows with us. Jesus showed us by his life and teaching how God wants human life to be.

This part of the prayer is called the **_Epiclesis_**, which means the summoning (calling) of the Holy Spirit. The Church everywhere includes this in the Eucharistic Prayer. Please join in putting your arms out towards the bread and the wine.

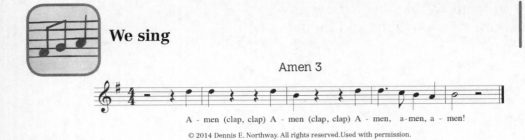

We sing

Amen 3

A - men (clap, clap) A - men (clap, clap) A - men, a-men, a - men!

© 2014 Dennis E. Northway. All rights reserved. Used with permission.

The Lord's Prayer

Presider: As our Savior Jesus Christ has taught us we now pray.

Assembly: Our Father in heaven, hallowed be your Name, your kingdom come, your will be done, on earth as it is in heaven. Give us today our daily bread. Forgive us our sins as we forgive those who sin against us. Save us from the time of trial; and deliver us from evil. For the kingdom, the power and the glory are yours, now and forever. Amen.

This is known as the "Great Amen." **Amen** means "yes" or "so be it!" or "yes, I agree God!"

The Breaking of the Bread

This bread is broken for us, we sing and we share communion with one another. We give the bread and say, "The Body of Christ (the Bread of Heaven)." We give the wine and say, "The Blood of Christ (the Cup of Salvation)."

We sing *(Please see songbook.)*

A Final Prayer and A Blessing

Member of the Assembly or Presider: God we thank you for feeding us with this spiritual food and for your promise that we are children of God and saved by Jesus.

Assembly: Amen!

Presider: May the blessing of the God of Abraham and Sarah, and of Jesus Christ our Good Shepherd, born of our sister Mary, and of the Holy Spirit, who broods over the world as a mother hen over her chicks, be upon you and remain with you always.

Assembly: Amen!

The Priest offers God's blessings, God's divine protection, and God's thanks for the Assembly gathered.

Sending Us Into the World

Deacon: Go in peace, to love and serve the Lord.
Assembly: Thanks be to God!

The Deacon (Helper) dismisses the Assembly.

The Rite Place

Maundy Thursday & Good Friday for Children

Welcome!

This liturgy is specifically designed for children and all in their households. Children (and adults) are active participants in an informal and relaxed setting wherein children are celebrated just as they are.

We are a church who firmly believes that all of God's children are welcome at the table of God. The liturgy is at the heart of all we do. From the full services on Sundays, to weekdays and the great feasts and seasons in the church year, we reach deeply into the riches of our Anglican tradition, building on it to explore new ways to give glory to God in our prayer, preaching and music.

We, like many others, find that when you speak directly to children, everyone listens. In this service, the teaching, the songs and the prayers will be aimed at the hearts and minds of our youngest worshippers, and all will learn something each week about the God who loves us.

We pray that this experience will be a wonderful way to connect adults with young children, and young children with adults. We strive to build a community where all feel a sense of hope and compassion from a church that welcomes all of God's children.

Three Days*

The Three Days (or Triduum) slow down time as we move through the climax of the story of faith, Jesus' betrayal, death, and resurrection. Worship throughout the rest of the year skims the surface in some ways, whisking us through the story of Jesus' life. But in these three days we linger. There is so much centered here. We have to take our time to be able to receive it.

Worship on these three days will cover it all: creation and redemption, death and life, fire and water, desolation and celebration. These days enact the great Christian drama, and the liturgies are, in many ways, dramas that embody the story, the tensions, and the teachings at the core of our faith.

The Triduum liturgies are, in effect, one continuous rite spread over three consecutive days. Thus, there is no blessing or dismissal until the conclusion of the First Mass of the Resurrection on Easter Eve at the Great Vigil of Easter.

Maundy Thursday

This evening marks the beginning of the Triduum. We reach back to the beginning of Lent to recall the confession we made on Ash Wednesday. This service is clearly different from the regular flow of the Eucharist as we celebrate it weekly, because what we commemorate this evening is different. Tonight we begin a celebration that will not end until the exultant conclusion of the Great Paschal Vigil. Tonight, we hear the words of forgiveness in a new way. It is only with the knowledge of being forgiven that we can engage the rest of the story. We watch and we eat a last supper with Jesus. We hear him offer all of himself to us, even his body and blood. We end the service with the stripping of the chancel. Adornment after adornment leaves the sanctuary as the words of the psalm drift through the air, and we are reminded of what this love will cost Jesus. We leave the service lingering. It is holy time.

Good Friday

We are now in the sanctuary on Good Friday and hours have passed. We will hear of Jesus' humiliation, his crucifixion. We know the night was long for him; it was probably very lonely. In front of us is the cross. There is nothing else to distract us. The pace is slow, as those final hours must have been for Jesus. Tonight we pray for the world around us, for our church, and ourselves. We will, like Jesus, pass through death on the way to Resurrection.

The Great Vigil of Easter

Now we are almost there, almost at the hour when Jesus' death itself was overcome, when death became life—the victory we so need. Now time stands still for us to remember all that has gone before. No other service is so full of the heritage of faith; no other time in the year do we gather together all of the richest metaphors and symbols of faith. We gather around new fire, itself a sign of creation renewed. From it we light the Paschal candle to illumine our way. As the pillar of fire led the people of Israel in the wilderness, so the Paschal candle will lead us to Easter—the light of Christ our beacon. In the silence from Good Friday, the light is rekindled. Gathered around the light, we wrap the great stories of faith like a blanket around ourselves. We recall our ancestors and God's saving work among us throughout the ages—creation from a word, the earth washed clean in the flood, the deliverance at the Red Sea, dry bones given life again. The baptismal font beckons to affirm our baptisms, to remember our welcome into the community of faith, and to welcome others newborn into the faith. The Gospel reading draws us out of our holy recollections and into the events of the story again. Now we are prepared. We know where we have come from before we peek into the tomb with the women and Peter. When we hear the angel say, "He is not here, but has risen", we know again that life is always God's way with us. Death is defeated. We dance through the holy meal, now each one confessing the truth of the story. Light the church! Shout Alleluia! Celebrate with high praise! He is risen!

*Adapted from *Sundays and Seasons 2004* (Minneapolis: AugsburgFortress, 2003), pp. 158-159.

Please join us on Saturday evening for the Great Vigil of Easter.

Watch for these symbols and meanings:

Procession	Shofar	Music	Crosses	Bell
Prayer	Bible Readings	Communion	Welcome & Dismissal	Holy Spirit

Maundy Thursday Service for Children

Welcome
We continue the Holy Week journey.

Gathering Song

We gather in the name of the God three-in-one or the Triune God, at the entrance to the church. We say hello to God and one another. We take time to see and welcome our neighbor.

We prepare.

We Are the Family Tree of God

Voice

We are the fam'-ly tree of God, We are the fam'-ly tree of God,

We are the fam'-ly tree of God, We are the fam'-ly tree of God.

A Gathering Time

Member or Presider of the Assembly: Blessed be the God who created us, loves us, and brought his Son Jesus to us.
Assembly: Glory to God for ever and ever. Amen.

Presider: Let us now process to the Foot Washing Station.

Can you find the bowl and water?

The Procession

We sing

Blessed Are the Pure in Heart for They Shall See God

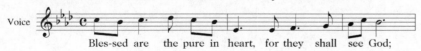

Voice

Bles-sed are the pure in heart, for they shall see God;

bles-sed are the pure in heart for they shall see God.

We Begin to Pray
The Collect of the Day

Member or Presider of the Assembly: God is with you.
Assembly: God is also with you.

Member or Presider of the Assembly: Let us pray.

Almighty God, whose dear Son, on the night before he suffered, instituted the Sacrament of his Body and Blood: Mercifully grant that we may receive it thankfully in remembrance of Jesus Christ our Lord, who in these holy mysteries gives us a pledge of eternal life; and who now lives and reigns with you and the Holy Spirit, one God, for ever and ever. **Amen**.

This prayer is called the Collect. The Leader or Priest "collects" or "gathers" the themes of the lesson, the church season, and the congregation into one prayer.

The Word of God: God Speaks.

We Listen and Respond.

Deacon: The Good News about Jesus as told by
_____.

The Deacon (or someone else) tells us the story about Jesus washing the disciples' feet.

Gospel Refrain
Assembly:

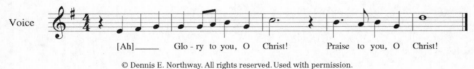

[Ah]____ Glo-ry to you, O Christ! Praise to you, O Christ!

© Dennis E. Northway. All rights reserved. Used with permission.

After the Gospel, the Deacon says: This is the Good News of the Good Shepherd.

We sing the *Gospel Refrain* again.

Homily

We talk about the scripture reading and what it means for us and how we live our lives.

The sound of the bell calls us to a moment of silence.

The Foot Washing

Presider: Fellow servants of our Lord Jesus Christ: On the night before his death, Jesus set an example for his disciples by washing their feet, an act of humble service. He taught that strength and growth in the life of the Kingdom of God comes not by power, authority, or even miracle, but by lowly service, and he commanded them to follow his example by washing one another's feet. Therefore, I invite you who share in the royal priesthood of Christ to come forward, that we may follow the example of our Master and remember the new commandment that he gave this night, "Love one another as I have loved you. By this shall the world know that you are my disciples: That you love one another."

As we wash each other's feet we sing together...

What does water do for us? What does it mean when we wash each other's feet? Jesus must have been refreshed!

We're Gathered in an Ash-filled Lent

Sung responsively

Voice

We're gath-ered in an ash-filled Lent with Je-sus as our bro-ther,

On Maun-dy Thurs-day Je-sus spent time wash-ing the feet of one an-o - ther.

He broke the bread and blessed the wine to show love for his chil-dren,

We share to-ge-ther in that sign a key part of gos-pel tra-di - tion.

The sound of the bell calls us to silent prayer.

The Peace

The Announcements

We shake hands with those around us and say "Peace" or "The Peace of the Lord be with you."

The Preparation of the Table and the Presentation of the Offerings

> *Member of the Assembly:* A gift is something we give; it is also something we are. It is time to give gifts of love, gifts of bread, gifts of money.

> **We sing** *(Please see songbook.) As we sing, the Deacon (Helper), the Priest (Elder) and some of our young seekers prepare the table.*

> *The sound of the bell calls us to silent prayer.*

The Holy Eucharist:

The Story of Jesus' meal with his friends.

Eucharist means "giving thanks" and here we give thanks for all the gifts God has given to us. We give some of our money to help the church do God's work. When we do this, we are saying that we do try to understand that all we have comes as a gift from God, including our money.

The Great Thanksgiving

Presider: The Lord is with you.
Assembly: The Lord is also with you.

Presider: Lift up your hearts.
Assembly: We lift them to the Lord.

Presider: Let us give thanks to the Lord our God.
Assembly: It is right to give God thanks and praise.

Presider: We praise you and we bless you, holy and gracious God, source of wisdom, light and hope.

We sing

Lord, You Are Holy (Sanctus)

Voice: Lord you are ho - ly. You are a God of power. You

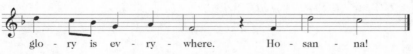

glo - ry is ev - ry - where. Ho - san - na!

Presider: On the night he was handed over to suffering and death, Jesus gathered his friends, he took the bread, blessed and broke it and gave it to his friends and said,

Assembly: "This is my body. Whenever you eat this do this in remembrance of me."

Presider: Then Jesus took the cup filled with wine, raised it up and gave thanks for it, shared it with his friends and said,

Assembly: "This is my blood. Whenever you drink this, do this in remembrance of me."

Presider: We offer you these gifts,

Assembly: Jesus, the bread of life. Jesus, the cup of salvation.

Presider: Jesus Christ has died.
Assembly: Jesus Christ has died.
Presider: Jesus Christ has risen.
Assembly: Jesus Christ has risen.
Presider: Jesus Christ will come again.
Assembly: Jesus Christ will come again.

Presider: Send your Holy Spirit upon us and upon these gifts.

Assembly: Let them be for us the Body and Blood of your Son.

Presider: And grant that we who eat this bread and drink this cup may be filled with your life and goodness.

We sing

We join with the priest in blessing this meal. Feel free to join in the movements of the priest.

We say the bold words together.

In this prayer, we especially remember that God became human in Jesus, so that he could share our joys and sorrows with us. Jesus showed us by his life and teaching how God wants human life to be.

This part of the prayer is called the **Epiclesis**, which means the summoning (calling) of the Holy Spirit. The Church everywhere includes this in the Eucharistic Prayer. Please join in putting your arms out towards the bread and the wine.

This is known as the "Great Amen." **Amen** means "yes" or "so be it!" or "yes, I agree God!"

Amen 3

A - men (clap, clap) A - men (clap, clap) A - men, a-men, a - men!

The Lord's Prayer

Presider: As our Savior Jesus Christ has taught us we now pray.

Assembly: Our Father in heaven, hallowed be your Name, your kingdom come, your will be done, on earth as it is in heaven. Give us today our daily bread. Forgive us our sins as we forgive those who sin against us. Save us from the time of trial; and deliver us from evil. For the kingdom, the power and the glory are yours, now and forever. Amen.

The Breaking of the Bread

This bread is broken for us, we sing and we share communion with one another. We give the bread and say, "The Body of Christ (the Bread of Heaven)." We give the wine and say, "The Blood of Christ (the Cup of Salvation)."

We sing *(Please see songbook.)*

The Clearing and Washing of the Altar

The sound of the bell calls us to silent prayer.

We quietly watch the Deacon clear the altar in preparation for Good Friday.

Member or Presider of the Assembly: When they had sung the hymn, they went out to the Mount of Olives.

We quietly listen to the story of what happened to Jesus next. Our service stops here quietly and will continue tomorrow.

Then Jesus said to them, "You will all become deserters because of me this night; for it is written, 'I will strike the shepherd, and the sheep of the flock will be scattered.' But after I am raised up I will go ahead of you to Galilee." Peter said to him, "Though all become deserters because of you, I will never desert you." Jesus said to him, "Truly I tell you, this very night, before the cock crows, you will deny me three times." Peter said to him, "Even though I must die with you, I will not deny you." And so said all the disciples.

Then Jesus went with them to a place called Gethsemane; and he said to his disciples, "Sit here while I go over there and pray." He took with him

Peter and the two sons of Zebedee, and began to be grieved and agitated. Then he said to them, "I am deeply grieved, even to death; remain here, and stay awake with me."

And going a little farther, he threw himself on the ground and prayed, "My Father, if it is possible, let this cup pass from me; yet not what I want but what you want." Then he came to the disciples and found them sleeping; and he said to Peter, "So, could you not stay awake with me one hour? Stay awake and pray that you may not come into the time of trial; the spirit indeed is willing, but the flesh is weak."

Again he went away for the second time and prayed, "My Father, if this cannot pass unless I drink it, your will be done." Again he came and found them sleeping, for their eyes were heavy. So leaving them again, he went away and prayed for the third time, saying the same words. Then he came to the disciples and said to them, "Are you still sleeping and taking your rest? See, the hour is at hand, and the Son of Man is betrayed into the hands of sinners. Get up; let us be going. See, my betrayer is at hand."

Join us tomorrow to continue
this three-day service of the Triduum.

A Good Friday Service for Children

Tonight we do not wander,
Tonight we do not roam,
This cross is our story,
This place is our home.

Tonight it is time to just sit and be quiet.

This cross is just a cross, but
What happened on this cross might be the most important
Thing in all our life!

As we return to the sanctuary on Good Friday, hours have passed. We hear of Jesus' humiliation, his crucifixion. We know the night was long for him, and lonely. Our visual center is the cross of which we gather around this evening. There is nothing else to distract us. The pace is slow, as those final hours must have been for Jesus. We move relentlessly toward the end. We pray, interceding for the world around us, for our church, and ourselves. We are reminded that Jesus, like us, passes from life through death on the way to Resurrection.

We Sing
(Cantor, then all):

Glo-ry be to Je - sus, pun-ished on a cross. He was just a vic-tim, such a bit - ter loss!

We talk about being punished for doing what was right.

We Sing
(Cantor, then all):

Glo-ry be to Je - sus, in - no-cent He was. Loved us lit - tle child - ren; gives His life, He does.

We Begin to Pray

The Collect of the Day

Member or Presider of the Assembly: God is with you.

Assembly: God is also with you.

This prayer is called the Collect. The Leader or Priest "collects" or "gathers" the themes of the lesson, the church season, and the congregation into one prayer.

Member or Presider of the Assembly: Let us pray.

Jesus, we gather because you rose from the tomb and you save us! By your Holy Spirit, strengthen and care for us as children of the Resurrection. **Amen**.

The Word of God: God Speaks.
We Listen and Respond.

A Story from the Gospel of John

The Deacon reads the account of the Crucifixion from John 19:16b-30.

Homily

We talk about the scripture reading and what it means for us and how we live our lives.

The sound of the bell calls us to a moment of silence.

We Sing
(Cantor, then all):

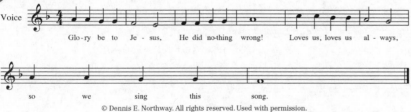

Glo-ry be to Je - sus, He did no-thing wrong! Loves us, loves us al - ways,

so we sing this song.

We Pray the Prayers of the People

Deacon: This is a special prayer. Please say after me:
We need to know LOVE is there always, always, always;
in sad times
in happy times
in quiet times
in birthday times
in bath-time times
in cleaning up your room times
in setting the table times
in going to church times

God is LOVE. It is promised in scripture. In the Eastern Orthodox tradition, it is not a Christian's aspiration to be like God, it is the Christian's aspiration to become God.

in catechesis times
in just plain every day times.

Jesus loves you
And all of us—
Your church FAMILY—
Love you too.

We Sing
(Cantor, then all):

Voice

Glo-ry be to Je - sus! on Good Fri-day's day! His love is our sto - ry,

by Him we will stay!

Tonight the story is not over. It continues to its triumphant climax tomorrow. Tonight, after we sing, we leave in silence.

We Sing

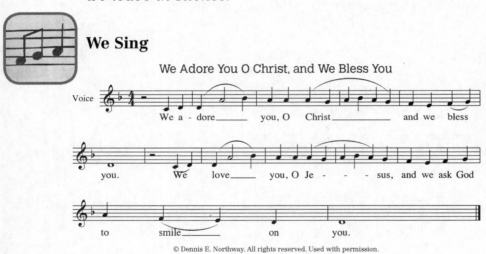

We Adore You O Christ, and We Bless You

Voice

We a - dore____ you, O Christ____ and we bless

you. We love____ you, O Je - - - sus, and we ask God

to smile____ on you.

To **bless** has many, many definitions, but one that might be most helpful and quite correct is to call God to smile on you.

Feel free to move up to the cross to pray by touching the cross or pausing or kneeling.

We hope you'll join us for the rest of the Triduum:
On Saturday at the Great Vigil of Easter
and on Easter Sunday

The Rite Place
Eastertide

Welcome!

This liturgy is specifically designed for children and all in their households. Children (and adults) are active participants in an informal and relaxed setting wherein children are celebrated just as they are.

We are a church who firmly believes that all of God's children are welcome at the table of God. The liturgy is at the heart of all we do. From the full services on Sundays, to weekdays and the great feasts and seasons in the church year, we reach deeply into the riches of our Anglican tradition, building on it to explore new ways to give glory to God in our prayer, preaching and music.

We, like many others, find that when you speak directly to children, everyone listens. In this service, the teaching, the songs and the prayers will be aimed at the hearts and minds of our youngest worshippers, and all will learn something each week about the God who loves us.

We pray that this experience will be a wonderful way to connect adults with young children, and young children with adults. We strive to build a community where all feel a sense of hope and compassion from a church that welcomes all of God's children.

Eastertide

"Christ is risen! He is risen indeed!" This is what we shout and this is what we believe! We are Easter people! Jesus suffered, died and rose from the dead. Jesus loves us so very much he gave everything for us. We, loved by Jesus Christ, wish to reach out to the world in love. Each of us can make a difference in the world; we can make it a better place. We gather to pray and praise and then we go out into the world rejoicing in our friendship and in the love of Christ. "Christ is risen! He is risen indeed!"

Watch for these symbols and meanings:

Procession   Shofar   Music   Crosses   Bell

Prayer   Bible Readings   Communion   Welcome & Dismissal   Holy Spirit

**We gather with our questions
as spiritual seekers on a journey.**

We gather to find God.

A Gathering Time

Welcome

We gather in the name of the God three-in-one or the Triune God, at the entrance to the church. We say hello to God and one another. We take time to see and welcome our neighbor.

We prepare.

Sounding of the Shofar

Israel used the ram's horn, called a shofar, to call together the people of God.

Member or Presider of the Assembly: Alleluia! Christ is risen!
Assembly: The Lord is risen indeed. Alleluia!

Opening Song

We sing a gathering song and process down the center aisle.

The Procession

Please feel free to carry an instrument, streamer, cross, or candle as we walk down the aisle. Place these objects in the wicker baskets when we approach and surround the table.

We Begin to Pray
The Collect of the Day

This prayer is called the Collect. The Leader or Priest "collects" or "gathers" the themes of the lesson, the church season, and the congregation into one prayer.

Member or Presider of the Assembly: God is with you.
Assembly: God is also with you.

Member or Presider of the Assembly: Let us pray.

Jesus, we gather because you rose from the tomb and you save us! By your Holy Spirit, strengthen and care for us as children of the Resurrection. **Amen.**

The Word of God: God Speaks.

We Listen and Respond.

 We sing

(The song will be announced.)

 A Story from the Hebrew Bible (Old Testament) or New Testament

Reader: Hear what the Spirit is saying to God's people.
Assembly: Thanks be to God.

or

Deacon: The Good News about Jesus as told by

_____.

Gospel Refrain
Assembly:

Voice

[Ah]____ Glo - ry to you, O Christ! Praise to you, O Christ!

After the Gospel, the Deacon says: This is the Good News of the Good Shepherd.

The Old Testament is also known as the Hebrew Bible, and contains the books that were written before Jesus was born. The New Testament contains the Gospels and Epistles (letters) and the Book of Acts written by a person who knew about Jesus.

The Deacon (or someone else) tells us the story found in the Gospel appointed for this Sunday of the Church Year. This reading is always from one of four books, Matthew, Mark, Luke or John found in the Bible.

 We sing the *Gospel Refrain* again.

 Homily

 The sound of the bell calls us to a moment of silence.

Baptismal Promises (optional)

Adult in the assembly: Will you continue to learn from the apostles' teaching, and break bread and pray together?
Assembly: I will, with God's help. Amen!

Adult in the assembly: Will you try and try to resist evil, and, whenever bad things happen or you do bad things, say you're sorry and turn again to the Lord?
Assembly: I will, with God's help. Amen!

Child in the assembly: Will you always show and tell Jesus to others?
Assembly: I will, with God's help. Amen!

Adult/Child: Will you seek and serve Jesus, love yourself and others as Jesus does?
Assembly: I will, with God's help. Amen!

Deacon: Will you strive for justice and peace among all people, and respect the dignity of everybody?
Assembly: I will, with God's help. Amen!

We Pray the Prayers of the People

Deacon: Let's join together in prayer, either out loud or quietly.

Leader: Let us take a moment to tell God "thank you" for all the good things that happen in our lives. Are there any special things we are grateful for? *(Pause)*

Leader: We say, "Thank you so much, Lord."
Assembly: Thank you so much, Lord.

Leader: Let us pray for those people or animals who are sick or who have died. *(Pause)*

Leader: We say, "God is with them."
Assembly: God is with them.

One of the most ancient acts of the Church is referred to as Intercessory Prayer. It is also one of the most holy. Holy means "set apart" or for very special use. Prayer is very, very special.

We ask God to help us and the people we care about. We give thanks for God's love for us and for those whom we love.

Please feel free to name things aloud or silently, any time during our prayer time.

We sing *(Please see songbook.)*

The Peace

The Announcements

Member of the Assembly: A gift is something we give; it is also something we are. It is time to give gifts of love, gifts of bread, gifts of money.

The Preparation of the Table and the Presentation of the Offerings

We sing *(Please see songbook.) As we sing, the Deacon (Helper), the Priest (Elder) and some of our young seekers prepare the table.*

The sound of the bell calls us to silent prayer.

The Holy Eucharist:

The Great Thanksgiving

Presider: The Lord is with you.
Assembly: The Lord is also with you.

Presider: Lift up your hearts.
Assembly: We lift them to the Lord.

Presider: Let us give thanks to the Lord our God.
Assembly: It is right to give God thanks and praise.

Presider: We praise you and we bless you, holy and gracious God, source of wisdom, light and hope.

We sing

We shake hands with those around us and say "Peace" or "The Peace of the Lord be with you."

The Story of Jesus' meal with his friends.

Eucharist means "giving thanks" and here we give thanks for all the gifts God has given to us. We give some of our money to help the church do God's work. When we do this, we are saying that we do try to understand that all we have comes as a gift from God, including our money.

Lord, You Are Holy (Sanctus)

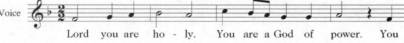

Lord you are ho - ly. You are a God of power. You

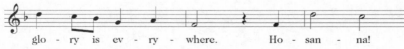

glo - ry is ev - ry - where. Ho - san - na!

Presider: On the night he was handed over to suffering and death, Jesus gathered his friends, he took the bread, blessed and broke it and gave it to his friends and said,

Assembly: "This is my body. Whenever you eat this do this in remembrance of me."

Presider: Then Jesus took the cup filled with wine, raised it up and gave thanks for it, shared it with his friends and said,

Assembly: "This is my blood. Whenever you drink this, do this in remembrance of me."

Presider: We offer you these gifts,

Assembly: Jesus, the bread of life. Jesus, the cup of salvation.

Presider: Jesus Christ has died.
Assembly: Jesus Christ has died.
Presider: Jesus Christ has risen.
Assembly: Jesus Christ has risen.
Presider: Jesus Christ will come again.
Assembly: Jesus Christ will come again.

Presider: Send your Holy Spirit upon us and upon these gifts.

Assembly: Let them be for us the Body and Blood of your Son.

Presider: And grant that we who eat this bread and drink this cup may be filled with your life and goodness.

We sing

We join with the priest in blessing this meal. Feel free to join in the movements of the priest.

We say the bold words together.

In this prayer, we especially remember that God became human in Jesus, so that he could share our joys and sorrows with us. Jesus showed us by his life and teaching how God wants human life to be.

This part of the prayer is called the **_Epiclesis_**, which means the summoning (calling) of the Holy Spirit. The Church everywhere includes this in the Eucharistic Prayer. Please join in putting your arms out towards the bread and the wine.

This is known as the "Great Amen." **_Amen_** means "yes" or "so be it!" or "yes, I agree God!"

Amen 1

With unrestrained joy!

Voice

A - men, A - men, A - men! (CLAP) A - men, A - men, A - men! (HEY!)

The Lord's Prayer

Presider: As our Savior Jesus Christ has taught us we now pray.

Assembly: Our Father in heaven, hallowed be your Name, your kingdom come, your will be done, on earth as it is in heaven. Give us today our daily bread. Forgive us our sins as we forgive those who sin against us. Save us from the time of trial; and deliver us from evil. For the kingdom, the power and the glory are yours, now and forever. Amen.

The Breaking of the Bread

This bread is broken for us, we sing and we share communion with one another. We give the bread and say, "The Body of Christ (the Bread of Heaven)." We give the wine and say, "The Blood of Christ (the Cup of Salvation)."

We sing *(Please see songbook.)*

A Final Prayer and A Blessing

Member of the Assembly or Presider: Let us pray.
Assembly: God we thank you for feeding us with this spiritual food and for your promise that we are children of God and saved by Jesus. Amen!

Presider: May the blessing of the God of Abraham and Sarah, and of Jesus Christ our Good Shepherd, born of our sister Mary, and of the Holy Spirit, who broods over the world as a mother hen over her chicks, be upon you and remain with you always.
Assembly: Amen!

The Priest offers God's blessings, God's divine protection, and God's thanks for the Assembly gathered.

Sending Us Into the World

Deacon: Alleluia! Christ is risen!
Assembly: The Lord is risen indeed! Alleluia!

The Deacon (Helper) dismisses the Assembly.

The Rite Place
The Season of Pentecost

Welcome!

This liturgy is specifically designed for children and all in their households. Children (and adults) are active participants in an informal and relaxed setting wherein children are celebrated just as they are.

We are a church who firmly believes that all of God's children are welcome at the table of God. The liturgy is at the heart of all we do. From the full services on Sundays, to weekdays and the great feasts and seasons in the church year, we reach deeply into the riches of our Anglican tradition, building on it to explore new ways to give glory to God in our prayer, preaching and music.

We, like many others, find that when you speak directly to children, everyone listens. In this service, the teaching, the songs and the prayers will be aimed at the hearts and minds of our youngest worshippers, and all will learn something each week about the God who loves us.

We pray that this experience will be a wonderful way to connect adults with young children, and young children with adults. We strive to build a community where all feel a sense of hope and compassion from a church that welcomes all of God's children.

The Season of Pentecost

The "Sundays after Pentecost," you might ask: what are they? What are we doing here this morning? Like the water cycle, water going from ice to steam or gas and then to water, the church has a cycle as well. In a part of the year, we prepare for and then welcome Jesus into the world as a baby, and into our lives; that is called Advent and Christmas. We then learn about the life and works of Jesus when he was in ministry on this earth; this is called the season of Epiphany. During Epiphany we learn about his miracles and his life story. We then prepare for the end of his physical ministry on earth and prepare for one very Holy Week. This time of preparation is called Lent. We then walk with Jesus as he triumphantly enters Jerusalem, shares a very special meal with his followers, becomes betrayed, is crucified, and then RISES FROM THE DEAD! This is Holy Week and Easter! We are Easter people! We rejoice and share in Christ's resurrection each week as we gather to pray and praise.

Then, Jesus sent the Comforter, or the Holy Spirit to be with his followers. The day the Holy Spirit came is called Pentecost, and what a flaming day it was! When the Spirit came upon Jesus' followers, they were given great vitality and small tongues of fire were upon each disciple's head. We are now in the weeks after the feast of Pentecost. Some may say this part of the church year is not as exciting. Here though, is a golden opportunity to think about the church! This is the time to discover who we are and whose we are. This is the time to ask who the church is (hint: it is you and me) and how we can be Christ in a world that is often sad, dishonest, violent, unfair, unkind, and mean. Jesus said each of us should reach out to the world to make it a better place. In this season of Sundays after Pentecost we can imagine and live out new ways to change the world!

Watch for these symbols and meanings:

Procession   Shofar   Music   Crosses   Bell

Prayer   Bible Readings   Communion   Welcome & Dismissal   Holy Spirit

We gather with our questions as spiritual seekers on a journey.

We gather to find God.

A Gathering Time

 Welcome

We gather in the name of the God three-in-one or the Triune God, at the entrance to the church. We say hello to God and one another. We take time to see and welcome our neighbor.

We prepare.

 Sounding of the Shofar

Israel used the ram's horn, called a shofar, to call together the people of God.

Member or Presider of the Assembly: Welcome. Blessed be the great three in one! The Creator, the Good Shepherd, and the Breath of God.
Assembly: Glory to God for ever and ever. Amen.

 Opening Song

We sing a gathering song and process down the center aisle.

The Procession

Please feel free to carry an instrument, streamer, cross, or candle as we walk down the aisle. Place these objects in the wicker baskets when we approach and surround the table.

 We Begin to Pray

The Collect of the Day

Member or Presider of the Assembly: God is with you.
Assembly: God is also with you.

This prayer is called the Collect. The Leader or Priest "collects" or "gathers" the themes of the lesson, the church season, and the congregation into one prayer.

Member or Presider of the Assembly: Let us pray.

Jesus, we are gathered because you taught us how to be children of God. By your Holy Spirit, nurture us as your people of the Resurrection. **Amen**.

The Word of God: God Speaks.

We Listen and Respond.

We sing

(The song will be announced.)

A Story from the Hebrew Bible (Old Testament) or New Testament

Reader: Hear what the Spirit is saying to God's people.
Assembly: Thanks be to God.

or

Deacon: The Good News about Jesus as told by

_____.

Gospel Refrain
Assembly:

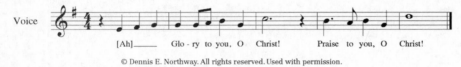

Voice   [Ah]_____   Glo - ry to you, O Christ!   Praise to you, O Christ!

© Dennis E. Northway. All rights reserved. Used with permission.

After the Gospel, the Deacon says: This is the Good News of the Good Shepherd.

The Old Testament is also known as the Hebrew Bible, and contains the books that were written before Jesus was born. The New Testament contains the Gospels and Epistles (letters) and the Book of Acts written by a person who knew about Jesus.

The Deacon (or someone else) tells us the story found in the Gospel appointed for this Sunday of the Church Year. This reading is always from one of four books, Matthew, Mark, Luke or John found in the Bible.

We sing the *Gospel Refrain* again.

Homily

We talk about the scripture reading and what it means for us and how we live our lives.

The sound of the bell calls us to a moment of silence.

We Pray the Prayers of the People

Deacon: Let's join together in prayer, either out loud or quietly.

Leader: Let us take a moment to tell God "thank you" for all the good things that happen in our lives. Are there any special things we are grateful for? *(Pause)*

Leader: We say, "Thank you so much, Lord."
Assembly: Thank you so much, Lord.

Leader: Let us pray for those people or animals who are sick or who have died. *(Pause)*

Leader: We say, "God is with them."
Assembly: God is with them.

Leader: Let us pray for people or situations that concern or worry us. *(Pause)*

Leader: We say, "Help us Lord, we trust in you."
Assembly: Help us Lord, we trust in you.

One of the most ancient acts of the Church is referred to as Intercessory Prayer. It is also one of the most holy. Holy means "set apart" or for very special use. Prayer is very, very special.

We ask God to help us and the people we care about. We give thanks for God's love for us and for those whom we love.

Please feel free to name things aloud or silently, any time during our prayer time.

We sing *(Please see songbook.)*

The Peace

The Announcements

We shake hands with those around us and say "Peace" or "The Peace of the Lord be with you."

The Preparation of the Table and the Presentation of the Offerings

Member of the Assembly: A gift is something we give; it is also something we are. It is time to give gifts of love, gifts of bread, gifts of money.

We sing *(Please see songbook.) As we sing, the Deacon (Helper), the Priest (Elder) and some of our young seekers prepare the table.*

The sound of the bell calls us to silent prayer.

The Holy Eucharist:

The Great Thanksgiving

Presider: The Lord is with you.
Assembly: The Lord is also with you.

Presider: Lift up your hearts.
Assembly: We lift them to the Lord.

Presider: Let us give thanks to the Lord our God.
Assembly: It is right to give God thanks and praise.

Presider: We praise you and we bless you, holy and gracious God, source of wisdom, light and hope.

We sing

Lord, You Are Holy (Sanctus)

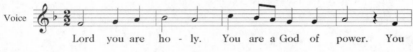

Lord you are ho - ly. You are a God of power. You

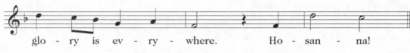

glo - ry is ev - ry - where. Ho - san - na!

Presider: On the night he was handed over to suffering and death, Jesus gathered his friends, he took the bread, blessed and broke it and gave it to his friends and said,
Assembly: "This is my body. Whenever you eat this do this in remembrance of me."

Presider: Then Jesus took the cup filled with wine, raised it up and gave thanks for it, shared it with his friends and said,
Assembly: "This is my blood. Whenever you drink this, do this in remembrance of me."

Presider: We offer you these gifts,
Assembly: Jesus, the bread of life. Jesus, the cup of salvation.

Presider: Jesus Christ has died.
Assembly: Jesus Christ has died.
Presider: Jesus Christ has risen.
Assembly: Jesus Christ has risen.
Presider: Jesus Christ will come again.

The Story of Jesus' meal with his friends.

Eucharist means "giving thanks" and here we give thanks for all the gifts God has given to us. We give some of our money to help the church do God's work. When we do this, we are saying that we do try to understand that all we have comes as a gift from God, including our money.

We join with the priest in blessing this meal. Feel free to join in the movements of the priest.

We say the bold words together.

In this prayer, we especially remember that God became human in Jesus, so that he could share our joys and sorrows with us. Jesus showed us by his life and teaching how God wants human life to be.

Assembly: Jesus Christ will come again.

Presider: Send your Holy Spirit upon us and upon these gifts.
Assembly: Let them be for us the Body and Blood of your Son.

Presider: And grant that we who eat this bread and drink this cup may be filled with your life and goodness.

We sing

This part of the prayer is called the ***Epiclesis***, which means the summoning (calling) of the Holy Spirit. The Church everywhere includes this in the Eucharistic Prayer. Please join in putting your arms out towards the bread and the wine.

This is known as the "Great Amen." ***Amen*** means "yes" or "so be it!" or "yes, I agree God!"

Amen 1

With unrestrained joy!

Voice

A - men, A - men, A - men! (CLAP) A - men, A - men, A - men! (HEY!)

© 2014 Dennis E. Northway. All rights reserved. Used with permission.

The Lord's Prayer

Presider: As our Savior Jesus Christ has taught us we now pray.
Assembly: Our Father in heaven, hallowed be your Name, your kingdom come, your will be done, on earth as it is in heaven. Give us today our daily bread. Forgive us our sins as we forgive those who sin against us. Save us from the time of trial; and deliver us from evil. For the kingdom, the power and the glory are yours, now and forever. Amen.

The Breaking of the Bread

This bread is broken for us, we sing and we share communion with one another. We give the bread and say, "The Body of Christ (the Bread of Heaven)." We give the wine and say, "The Blood of Christ (the Cup of Salvation)."

We sing *(Please see songbook.)*

A Final Prayer and A Blessing

Member of the Assembly or Presider: Let us pray.
Assembly: God we thank you for feeding us with this spiritual food and for your promise that we are children of God and saved by Jesus. Amen!

Presider: May the blessing of the God of Abraham and Sarah, and of Jesus Christ our Good Shepherd, born of our sister Mary, and of the Holy Spirit, who broods over the world as a mother hen over her chicks, be upon you and remain with you always.
Assembly: Amen!

The Priest offers God's blessings, God's divine protection, and God's thanks for the Assembly gathered.

Sending Us Into the World

Deacon: Go in peace, to love and serve the Lord.
Assembly: Thanks be to God!

The Deacon (Helper) dismisses the Assembly.

The Rite Place

Holy Baptism

Welcome!

This liturgy is specifically designed for children and all in their households. Children (and adults) are active participants in an informal and relaxed setting wherein children are celebrated just as they are.

We are a church who firmly believes that all of God's children are welcome at the table of God. The liturgy is at the heart of all we do. From the full services on Sundays, to weekdays and the great feasts and seasons in the church year, we reach deeply into the riches of our Anglican tradition, building on it to explore new ways to give glory to God in our prayer, preaching and music.

We, like many others, find that when you speak directly to children, everyone listens. In this service, the teaching, the songs and the prayers will be aimed at the hearts and minds of our youngest worshippers, and all will learn something each week about the God who loves us.

We pray that this experience will be a wonderful way to connect adults with young children, and young children with adults. We strive to build a community where all feel a sense of hope and compassion from a church that welcomes all of God's children.

Holy Baptism

When we gather as Christians, we seek to do the things Jesus did. Jesus broke bread with his disciples, so we break bread. Jesus helped the poor and the sick, so we strive to help people as well. Jesus was also baptized, and so we use Baptism to welcome people into the community of Christ. Just as the people of the Hebrew Scriptures (Old Testament) had a covenant or understanding of their relationship to God, we gather and make a covenant with a person who seeks to become part of the community of Christ. In the early church, Baptism and welcoming one into the church was an important life event and people often prepared for up to a year before becoming baptized. This was a time to learn about Jesus and the Christian life. Baptism is a formal initiation into the Body of Christ. Today, we ask a series of very important questions to the seeker wishing to become a member of the Body of Christ and to the parents and godparents who are presenting a child for baptism. We pray together and we ask the Holy Spirit to dwell deeply in their heart. As a community, we firmly commit, or covenant, with that person that we will live with them, walk with them, learn with them and be Christ with and for them.

Be sure to watch for these symbols during worship today: water, a baby or person to be baptized, a shell, the baptismal font, sponsors and parents, the gathered assembly, a candle, and a cloth. I wonder what they all mean.

Watch for these symbols and meanings:

Procession   Shofar   Music   Crosses   Bell

Prayer   Bible Readings   Communion   Welcome & Dismissal   Holy Spirit

**We gather with our questions
as spiritual seekers on a journey.**

We gather to find God.

A Gathering Time

Welcome

We gather in the name of the God three-in-one or the Triune God, at the entrance to the church. We say hello to God and one another. We take time to see and welcome our neighbor.

We prepare.

Sounding of the Shofar

Israel used the ram's horn, called a shofar, to call together the people of God.

Member of the Assembly: Blessed be God: Father, Son, and Holy Spirit.
Assembly: And blessed be God's kingdom, now and for ever. Amen.

Member of the Assembly: There is one Body and one Spirit;
Assembly: There is one hope in God's call to us;

Member of the Assembly: One Lord, one Faith, one Baptism;
Assembly: One God of all.

Opening Song

We sing a gathering song and process down the center aisle.

The Procession

Please feel free to carry an instrument, streamer, cross, or candle as we walk down the aisle. Place these objects in the wicker baskets when we approach and surround the table.

We Begin to Pray

The Collect of the Day

Member or Presider of the Assembly: God is with you.

Assembly: God is also with you.

Member or Presider of the Assembly: Let us pray.

Jesus, we are gathered because you lived, died and rose for us. By your Holy Spirit, nurture us as your people of the Resurrection. **Amen.**

This prayer is called the Collect. The Leader or Priest "collects" or "gathers" the themes of the lesson, the church season, and the congregation into one prayer.

The Word of God: God Speaks.

We Listen and Respond.

We sing

(The song will be announced.)

A Story from the Hebrew Bible (Old Testament) or New Testament

Reader: Hear what the Spirit is saying to God's people.

Assembly: Thanks be to God.

or

Deacon: The Good News about Jesus as told by

_____.

The Old Testament is also known as the Hebrew Bible, and contains the books that were written before Jesus was born. The New Testament contains the Gospels and Epistles (letters) and the Book of Acts written by a person who knew about Jesus.

Gospel Refrain
Assembly:

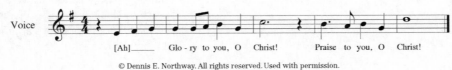

Voice

[Ah]_____ Glo-ry to you, O Christ! Praise to you, O Christ!

© Dennis E. Northway. All rights reserved. Used with permission.

The Deacon (or someone else) tells us the story found in the Gospel appointed for this Sunday of the Church Year. This reading is always from one of four books, Matthew, Mark, Luke or John found in the Bible.

After the Gospel, the Deacon says: This is the Good News of the Good Shepherd.

We sing the *Gospel Refrain* again.

Homily

We talk about the scripture reading and what it means for us and how we live our lives.

 The sound of the bell calls us to a moment of silence.

Baptismal Promises

 Adult in the assembly: Will you continue to learn from the apostles' teaching, and break bread and pray together?
Assembly: I will, with God's help. Amen!

Adult in the assembly: Will you try and try to resist evil, and, whenever bad things happen or you do bad things, say you're sorry and turn again to the Lord?
Assembly: I will, with God's help. Amen!

Child in the assembly: Will you always show and tell Jesus to others?
Assembly: I will, with God's help. Amen!

Adult/Child: Will you seek and serve Jesus, love yourself and others as Jesus does?
Assembly: I will, with God's help. Amen!

Deacon: Will you strive for justice and peace among all people, and respect the dignity of everybody?
Assembly: I will, with God's help. Amen!

 We sing *(Please see songbook.)*

The Peace

The Announcements

We shake hands with those around us and say "Peace" or "The Peace of the Lord be with you."

The Preparation of the Table and the Presentation of the Offerings

Member of the Assembly: A gift is something we give; it is also something we are. It is time to give gifts of love, gifts of bread, gifts of money.

We sing *(Please see songbook.) As we sing, the Deacon (Helper), the Priest (Elder) and some of our young seekers prepare the table.*

 The sound of the bell calls us to silent prayer.

The Holy Eucharist:

 The Great Thanksgiving

Presider: The Lord is with you.
Assembly: The Lord is also with you.

Presider: Lift up your hearts.
Assembly: We lift them to the Lord.

Presider: Let us give thanks to the Lord our God.
Assembly: It is right to give God thanks and praise.

Presider: We praise you and we bless you, holy and gracious God, source of wisdom, light and hope.

 We sing

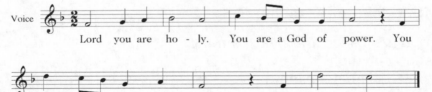

Lord, You Are Holy (Sanctus)

Lord you are ho-ly. You are a God of power. You glo-ry is ev-ry-where. Ho-san-na!

© 2009 Dennis E. Northway. All rights reserved. Used with permission.

 Presider: On the night he was handed over to suffering and death, Jesus gathered his friends, he took the bread, blessed and broke it and gave it to his friends and said,
Assembly: "This is my body. Whenever you eat this do this in remembrance of me."

Presider: Then Jesus took the cup filled with wine, raised it up and gave thanks for it, shared it with his friends and said,

The Story of Jesus' meal with his friends.

Eucharist means "giving thanks" and here we give thanks for all the gifts God has given to us. We give some of our money to help the church do God's work. When we do this, we are saying that we do try to understand that all we have comes as a gift from God, including our money.

We join with the priest in blessing this meal. Feel free to join in the movements of the priest.

We say the bold words together.

In this prayer, we especially remember that God became human in Jesus, so that he could share our joys and sorrows with us. Jesus showed us by his life and teaching how God wants human life to be.

Assembly: "This is my blood. Whenever you drink this, do this in remembrance of me."

Presider: We offer you these gifts,
Assembly: Jesus, the bread of life. Jesus, the cup of salvation.

Presider: Jesus Christ has died.
Assembly: Jesus Christ has died.
Presider: Jesus Christ has risen.
Assembly: Jesus Christ has risen.
Presider: Jesus Christ will come again.
Assembly: Jesus Christ will come again.

Presider: Send your Holy Spirit upon us and upon these gifts.
Assembly: Let them be for us the Body and Blood of your Son.

Presider: And grant that we who eat this bread and drink this cup may be filled with your life and goodness.

This part of the prayer is called the **Epiclesis**, which means the summoning (calling) of the Holy Spirit. The Church everywhere includes this in the Eucharistic Prayer. Please join in putting your arms out towards the bread and the wine.

We sing

This is known as the "Great Amen." **Amen** means "yes" or "so be it!" or "yes, I agree God!"

Amen 1

With unrestrained joy!

Voice

A - men, A - men, A - men! (CLAP) A - men, A - men, A - men! (HEY!)

The Lord's Prayer

Presider: As our Savior Jesus Christ has taught us we now pray.
Assembly: Our Father in heaven, hallowed be your Name, your kingdom come, your will be done, on earth as it is in heaven. Give us today our daily bread. Forgive us our sins as we forgive those who sin against us. Save us from the time of trial; and deliver us from evil. For the kingdom, the power and the glory are yours, now and forever. Amen.

The Breaking of the Bread

This bread is broken for us, we sing and we share communion with one another. We give the bread and say, "The Body of Christ (the Bread of Heaven)." We give the wine and say, "The Blood of Christ (the Cup of Salvation)."

 We sing *(Please see songbook.)*

A Final Prayer and A Blessing

 Member of the Assembly or Presider: God we thank you for feeding us with this spiritual food. Send us out into the world to be the people of God.
Assembly: Amen!
Presider: May the blessing of the God of Abraham and Sarah, and of Jesus Christ our Good Shepherd, born of our sister Mary, and of the Holy Spirit, who broods over the world as a mother hen over her chicks, be upon you and remain with you always.
Assembly: Amen!

The Priest offers God's blessings, God's divine protection, and God's thanks for the Assembly gathered.

Sending Us Into the World

 Deacon: Go in peace, to love and serve the Lord.
Assembly: Thanks be to God!

The Deacon (Helper) dismisses the Assembly.

The Rite Place

A Celebration of Life

Welcome!

This liturgy is specifically designed for children and all in their households. Children (and adults) are active participants in an informal and relaxed setting wherein children are celebrated just as they are.

We are a church who firmly believes that all of God's children are welcome at the table of God. The liturgy is at the heart of all we do. From the full services on Sundays, to weekdays and the great feasts and seasons in the church year, we reach deeply into the riches of our Anglican tradition, building on it to explore new ways to give glory to God in our prayer, preaching and music.

We, like many others, find that when you speak directly to children, everyone listens. In this service, the teaching, the songs and the prayers will be aimed at the hearts and minds of our youngest worshippers, and all will learn something each week about the God who loves us.

We pray that this experience will be a wonderful way to connect adults with young children, and young children with adults. We strive to build a community where all feel a sense of hope and compassion from a church that welcomes all of God's children.

A Celebration of Life

There are a couple of things that we are doing when we have a funeral. We are sad, because our friend or family member or pet isn't with us anymore, and so we are telling God and each other that we miss them. We are grateful, because our loved one has gone to be with God where we know they are peaceful and can rest, and so we are thanking God for caring so much about them. We are glad, because we have a lot of fun and happy memories of these people we love, so we are celebrating their lives and telling God how special they were to us. Funerals are special, because we do all of this together. At a funeral we gather together with the people who were important in our loved one's life, and share these feelings.

We are also remembering more than just our loved one at a funeral. When we have a funeral, especially when we have one on Sunday mornings alongside the rest of what we usually do in church, we are also remembering Jesus' death, and how he came back. When Jesus rose from the tomb on Easter, he taught us that God's love for us is more powerful than something scary like death. The miracle of the resurrection tells us that death is an important part of life, and that we don't need to be afraid because God is with us there, just as God is with us everywhere.

During today's service, we will remember our friend, share memories and maybe some tears. We will sing songs and hear stories about how much God loves us. We will say prayers that ask God to give us new life and keep our loved one safe in love and peace. At the end, we will say goodbye to our loved one, even though we know we will never forget him or her. "Alleluia, Christ is risen!" we will say. "The Lord is risen indeed." Alleluia!

Watch for these symbols and meanings:

Procession

Shofar

Music

Crosses

Bell

Prayer

Bible Readings

Communion

Welcome & Dismissal

Holy Spirit

**We gather with our questions
as spiritual seekers on a journey.**

We gather to find God.

A Gathering Time

Welcome

We gather in the name of the God three-in-one or the Triune God, at the entrance to the church. We say hello to God and one another. We take time to see and welcome our neighbor.

We prepare.

Sounding of the Shofar

Israel used the ram's horn, called a shofar, to call together the people of God.

Member or Presider of the Assembly: Welcome in the name of God: Creator, Shepherd, and Wind.
Assembly: Amen.

Member or Presider of the Assembly:
I am Resurrection and I am Life, says the Lord
Whoever has faith in me shall have life, even
   though he die.
And everyone who has life, and does my work and
   carries my light in faith, will live and be with
   God forever.

Opening Song

We sing a gathering song and process down the center aisle.

The Procession

Please feel free to carry an instrument, streamer, cross, or candle as we walk down the aisle. Place these objects in the wicker baskets when we approach and surround the table.

We Begin to Pray

The Collect of the Day

Member or Presider of the Assembly: God is with you.

Assembly: God is also with you.

Member or Presider of the Assembly: Let us pray.

O God of grace and glory, we remember before you this day our *brother/sister NAME*. We thank you for giving *him/her* to us, *his/her* family and friends, to know and to love as a friend on our earthly journey.

Presider: In your boundless compassion, console us who mourn.

This prayer is called the Collect. The Leader or Priest "collects" or "gathers" the themes of the lesson, the church season, and the congregation into one prayer.

The Word of God: God Speaks.

We Listen and Respond.

We sing

(The song will be announced.)

A Story from the Hebrew Bible (Old Testament) or New Testament

Reader: Hear what the Spirit is saying to God's people.
Assembly: Thanks be to God.

or

Deacon: The Good News about Jesus as told by

_____.

The Old Testament is also known as the Hebrew Bible, and contains the books that were written before Jesus was born. The New Testament contains the Gospels and Epistles (letters) and the Book of Acts written by a person who knew about Jesus.

The Deacon (or someone else) tells us the story found in the Gospel appointed for this Sunday of the Church Year. This reading is always from one of four books, Matthew, Mark, Luke or John found in the Bible.

Gospel Refrain
Assembly:

Voice

[Ah]_____ Glo - ry to you, O Christ! Praise to you, O Christ!

After the Gospel, the Deacon says: This is the Good News of the Good Shepherd.

We sing the Gospel Refrain again.

 Homily

We talk about the scripture reading and what it means for us and how we live our lives.

 The sound of the bell calls us to a moment of silence.

We Pray the Prayers of the People

 Deacon: It is time to pray to God. We join together to name our concerns or joys aloud or in quiet prayer.

Leader: Sometimes things go wrong, or we do wrong. We are sorry for them. Are there things for which we are sorry? *(Pause)*

Leader: We say, "Lord, we are sorry."
Assembly: Lord, we are sorry.

Leader: Let us take a moment to tell God "thank you" for all the just plain good things that happen in our lives. Are there any special things we are grateful for? *(Pause)*

Leader: We say, "Thank you so much, Lord."
Assembly: Thank you so much, Lord.

Leader: Let us pray for those people or animals who have died. *(Pause)*

Leader: We say, "God is with them."
Assembly: God is with them.

Leader: Sometimes we know people who are sick or we are worried about something in our lives. Are there any special needs, concerns or worries we should tell God about? *(Pause)*

Leader: We say, "Help us always, Lord."
Assembly: Help us always, Lord.

One of the most ancient acts of the Church is referred to as Intercessory Prayer. It is also one of the most holy. Holy means "set apart" or for very special use. Prayer is very, very special.

We ask God to help us and the people we care about. We give thanks for God's love for us and for those whom we love.

Please feel free to name things aloud or silently, any time during our prayer time.

Leader: For our brother (sister) *Name*, let us pray to our Lord Jesus Christ who said, "I am Resurrection and I am Life." Lord, you consoled Martha and Mary in their sadness; draw near to us who mourn for *Name*, and dry the tears of those who weep.
Assembly: Hear us, Lord.

Leader: Our brother (sister) was washed in Baptism and marked with the Holy Spirit; give him (her) company with all your saints.
Assembly: Hear us, Lord.

Assembly: Comfort us in our sadness at the death of our brother (sister); let our faith be our consolation, and eternal life our hope.

Presider: God of all, we pray to you for *Name*, and for all those whom we love but see no longer. Grant to them eternal rest. Let light perpetual shine upon them. May his (her) soul and the souls of all the departed, through the mercy of God, rest in peace. **Amen.**

 We sing *(Please see songbook.)*

The Peace

The Announcements

We shake hands with those around us and say "Peace" or "The Peace of the Lord be with you."

The Preparation of the Table and the Presentation of the Offerings

Member of the Assembly: A gift is something we give; it is also something we are. It is time to give gifts of love, gifts of bread, gifts of money.

 We sing *(Please see songbook.) As we sing, the Deacon (Helper), the Priest (Elder) and some of our young seekers prepare the table.*

 The sound of the bell calls us to silent prayer.

The Holy Eucharist:

The Story of Jesus' meal with his friends.

Eucharist means "giving thanks" and here we give thanks for all the gifts God has given to us. We give some of our money to help the church do God's work. When we do this, we are saying that we do try to understand that all we have comes as a gift from God, including our money.

The Great Thanksgiving

Presider: The Lord is with you.
Assembly: The Lord is also with you.

Presider: Lift up your hearts.
Assembly: We lift them to the Lord.

Presider: Let us give thanks to the Lord our God.
Assembly: It is right to give God thanks and praise.

Presider: We praise you and we bless you, holy and gracious God, source of wisdom, light and hope.

We sing

Lord, You Are Holy (Sanctus)

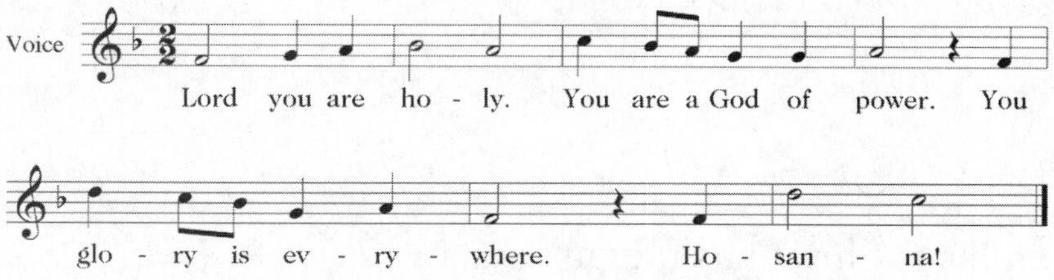
Voice
Lord you are ho - ly. You are a God of power. You
glo - ry is ev - ry - where. Ho - san - na!

© 2009 Dennis E. Northway. All rights reserved. Used with permission.

Presider: On the night he was handed over to suffering and death, Jesus gathered his friends, he took the bread, blessed and broke it and gave it to his friends and said,
Assembly: "This is my body. Whenever you eat this do this in remembrance of me."

Presider: Then Jesus took the cup filled with wine, raised it up and gave thanks for it, shared it with his friends and said,
Assembly: "This is my blood. Whenever you drink this, do this in remembrance of me."

Presider: We offer you these gifts,
Assembly: Jesus, the bread of life. Jesus, the cup of salvation.

Presider: Jesus Christ has died.
Assembly: Jesus Christ has died.
Presider: Jesus Christ has risen.
Assembly: Jesus Christ has risen.
Presider: Jesus Christ will come again.

We join with the priest in blessing this meal. Feel free to join in the movements of the priest.

We say the bold words together.

In this prayer, we especially remember that God became human in Jesus, so that he could share our joys and sorrows with us. Jesus showed us by his life and teaching how God wants human life to be.

Assembly: Jesus Christ will come again.

Presider: Send your Holy Spirit upon us and upon these gifts.
Assembly: Let them be for us the Body and Blood of your Son.

Presider: And grant that we who eat this bread and drink this cup may be filled with your life and goodness.

We sing

This part of the prayer is called the **Epiclesis**, which means the summoning (calling) of the Holy Spirit. The Church everywhere includes this in the Eucharistic Prayer. Please join in putting your arms out towards the bread and the wine.

This is known as the "Great Amen." **Amen** means "yes" or "so be it!" or "yes, I agree God!"

Amen 3

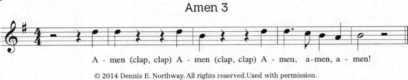

A - men (clap, clap) A - men (clap, clap) A - men, a-men, a - men!

The Lord's Prayer

Presider: As our Savior Jesus Christ has taught us we now pray.
Assembly: Our Father in heaven, hallowed be your Name, your kingdom come, your will be done, on earth as it is in heaven. Give us today our daily bread. Forgive us our sins as we forgive those who sin against us. Save us from the time of trial; and deliver us from evil. For the kingdom, the power and the glory are yours, now and forever. Amen.

The Breaking of the Bread

This bread is broken for us, we sing and we share communion with one another. We give the bread and say, "The Body of Christ (the Bread of Heaven)." We give the wine and say, "The Blood of Christ (the Cup of Salvation)."

We sing *(Please see songbook.)*

A Final Prayer and A Blessing

Member of the Assembly or Presider: **God we thank you for feeding us with this spiritual food and for your promise that we are children of God and saved by Jesus.**

Assembly: Amen!

Presider: Grant that this sacrament (this bread and wine) may be to us a comfort in hard times, and a promise that we are welcome in that kingdom where there is no death, neither sorrow nor crying, but the fullness of joy with all your saints; through Jesus Christ our Savior.

Assembly: Amen.

The Priest offers God's blessings, God's divine protection, and God's thanks for the Assembly gathered.

Sending Us Into the World

Assembly: Send us forth with a blessing.

Presider: Into paradise may the angels lead you. At your coming may the martyrs receive you, and bring you into the holy city Jerusalem. And the blessing of God Almighty, Creator, Shepherd, and Wind be upon you this day and ever more.

Deacon: Alleluia! Christ is risen!

Assembly: The Lord is risen indeed! Alleluia!

Deacon: Let us go forth in the name of Christ.

Assembly: Thanks be to God.

The Deacon (Helper) dismisses the Assembly.

Chapter 8:

The Song Book

All of the songs found here were composed for The Rite Place by Dennis Northway. You may use these songs for your own local congregation with The Rite Place liturgies. Please include a notice that you have the permission of Dennis Northway to reproduce these songs in your service folders as part of your ownership of The Rite Place, for congregational use.

ADVENT / CHRISTMAS / EPIPHANY

Jesus, You Are Light

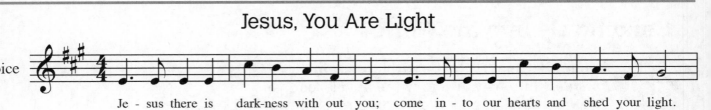

Je - sus there is dark-ness with out you; come in - to our hearts and shed your light.

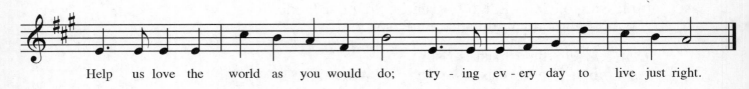

Help us love the world as you would do; try - ing ev - ery day to live just right.

Light Up My Heart

Light up my heart with your life - giv - ing Word; light up my soul with your

love. Light up my heart with your life - giv - ing Word; sent down to us from a -

bove!

Light to Scatter the Darkness!

Light to scat-ter the dark - ness! Light to show us the way!

Light to scat-ter the dark - ness! In our hearts Je - sus stay!

Prepare Me, O Lord

Pre - pare me, O Lord, pre - pare me, O Lord, pre - pare my heart, pre - pare my sou, pre-

pare me, pre - pare me oh Lord!

Tell the Watchmen the KING is Coming!

Tell the watch-men the KING is com-ing! Op - pen the doors!

Tell the watch-men the KING is com-ing! Op - en your hearts!

Bring Je_____ sus_____ in!

LENT

Ash Wednesday Song

Wa - ter that cleans, wa - ter that cleans wa - ter that cleans.

We Are in Lent

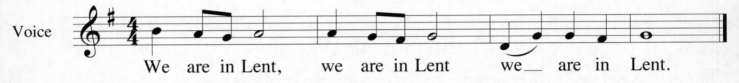

We are in Lent, we are in Lent we__ are in Lent.

PALM SUNDAY

Prepare the Way for the King!

A Round for Palm Sunday

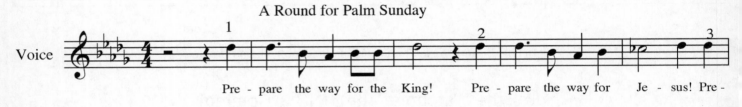

Pre - pare the way for the King! Pre - pare the way for Je - sus! Pre-

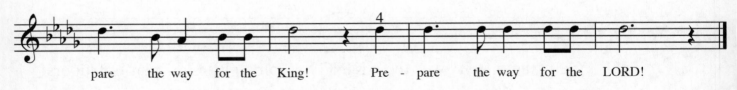

pare the way for the King! Pre - pare the way for the LORD!

MAUNDY THURSDAY

We're Gathered in an Ash-filled Lent

We're gath-ered in an ash-filled Lent with Je-sus as our bro-ther,

On Maun-dy Thurs-day Je-sus spent time wash-ing the feet of one an-o- - -ther.

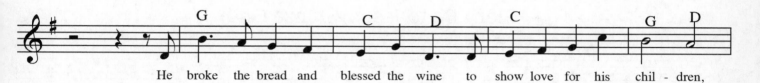

He broke the bread and blessed the wine to show love for his chil-dren,

We share to-ge-ther in that sign a key part of gos-pel tra-di- - -tion.

GOOD FRIDAY

Blessed Be, O Christ

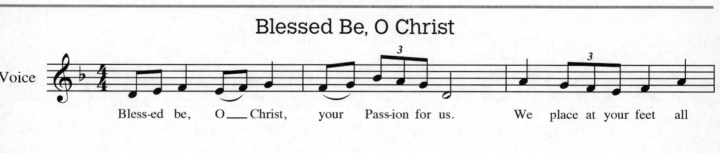

Bless-ed be, O___ Christ, your Pass-ion for us. We place at your feet all

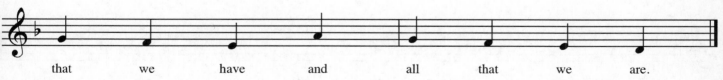

that we have and all that we are.

Glory Be to Jesus–refrain and three stanzas

Glo-ry be to Je - sus! on Good Fri-day's day! His love is our sto - ry,

by Him we will stay!

Glory Be to Jesus–Stanza One

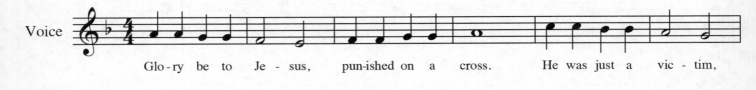

Glo-ry be to Je - sus, pun-ished on a cross. He was just a vic - tim,

such a bit - ter loss!

Glory Be to Jesus–Stanza Two

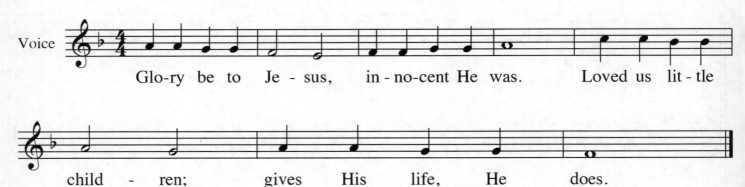

Glo-ry be to Je - sus, in - no-cent He was. Loved us lit - tle

child - ren; gives His life, He does.

Glory Be to Jesus–Stanza Three

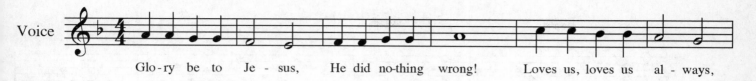

Glo-ry be to Je - sus, He did no-thing wrong! Loves us, loves us al - ways,

so we sing this song.

We Adore You O Christ, and We Bless You

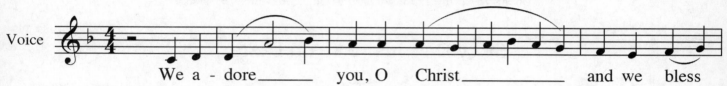

We a - dore_____ you, O Christ_____ and we bless

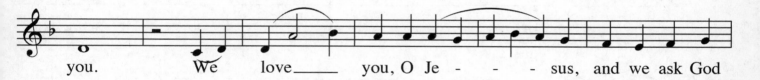

you. We love_____ you, O Je - - - sus, and we ask God

to smile_____ on you.

Easter Flowers

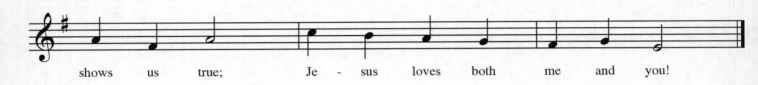

Ev'ry Day, Just Like on Easter!

Halleluia, Christ is Risen Again!

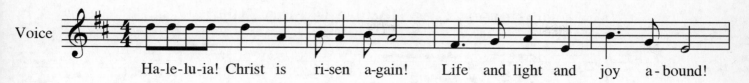

Ha-le-lu-ia! Christ is ri-sen a-gain! Life and light and joy a-bound!

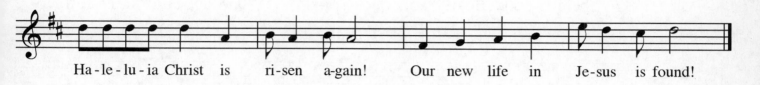

Ha-le-lu-ia Christ is ri-sen a-gain! Our new life in Je-sus is found!

PENTECOST

Stir Up the Flame

Stir up the flame, O Spi-rit God, and let the - Spi - rit shine in me! Stir up the

flame, O Spi - rit God and set your ser - vants free!_____

There Is One Body and One Spirit

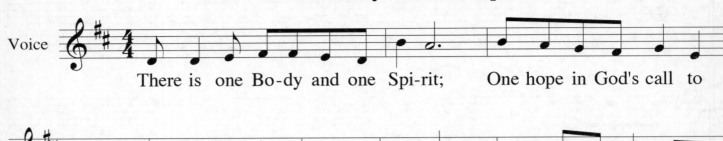

There is one Bo-dy and one Spi-rit; One hope in God's call to

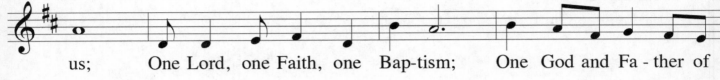

us; One Lord, one Faith, one Bap-tism; One God and Fa - ther of

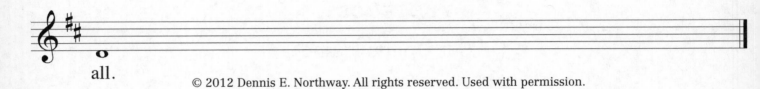

all.

We Thank You God for the Gift of Water

We thank you God for the gift of wa - ter; we

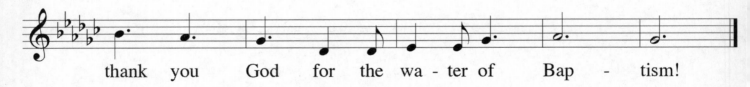

thank you God for the wa - ter of Bap - tism!

ROGATION AND PET BLESSING

Bless the Birds and Beasties Too!

Bless the birds and beas-ties too Bless the cats, and dogs and

bears, You know God loves them and you, knows you joys, your fears, your

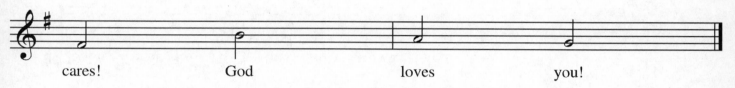

cares! God loves you!

These Are All a Gift from God

Leader All
are a gift from God!_____ are a gift from God!

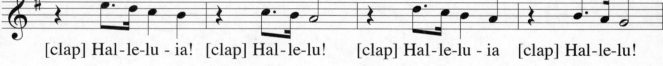

[clap] Hal-le-lu-ia! [clap] Hal-le-lu! [clap] Hal-le-lu-ia [clap] Hal-le-lu!

Some Options:

Brothers, Sisters, Mothers, Fathers, Children, Teachers, Pastors, Leaders, Babies, Kitties, Doggies, Critters, Grannies, Grandpas, Aunties, Uncles!

LITURGY SONGS (AMENS, SANCTUS, PRAYER RESPONSES)

Amen 1

With unrestrained joy!

A - men, A - men, A - men! (CLAP) A - men, A - men, A - men! (HEY!)

Amen 2

Exuberantly!

A - men! (CLAP CLAP) A - men! (CLAP CLAP CLAP)

A - men! A - men! A - men! [A]

Amen 3

A - men (clap, clap) A - men (clap, clap) A - men, a - men, a - men!

Glory To You, O Christ (Gospel Acclamation)

[Ah]_____ Glo - ry to you, O Christ! Praise to you, O Christ!

God, We Have Made You Glad. Bless Us.
(Prayers of the People response)

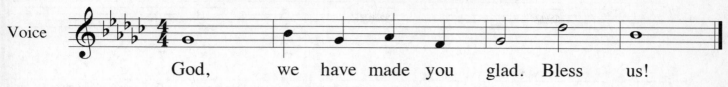

God, we have made you glad. Bless us!

God, We Have Made You Sad. Bless Us.
(Prayers of the People response)

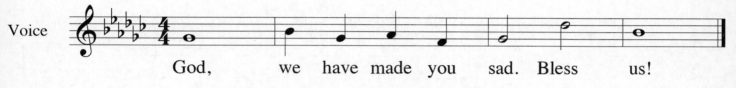

God, we have made you sad. Bless us!

Hear Our Prayer (Prayers of the People response)

Hear our prayer.

Hear Us, Good Lord (Prayers of the People response)

Hear us, good Lord, Hear us, good Lord. Ah!

Hear Us Lord of Light (Prayers of the People response)

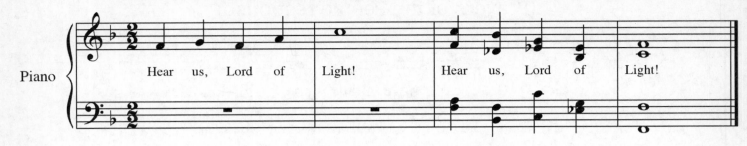

Piano

Hear us, Lord of Light! Hear us, Lord of Light!

Jubliate Deo

A Six-part round

Ju - bi - la - te De - o, ju - bi - la - te De - o, A - le - lu - ia!

N.B. This round is in public domain.

Kyrie

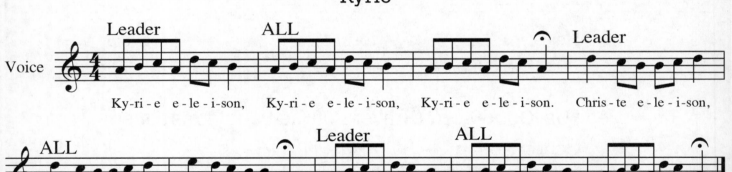

Voice

Ky-ri-e e-le-i-son, Ky-ri-e e-le-i-son, Ky-ri-e e-le-i-son. Chris-te e-le-i-son,

Chris-te e-le-i-son, Chris-te e-lei-son. Ky-ri-e e-le-i-son, Ky-ri-e e-le-i-son, Ky-ri-e e-le-i-son!

Kyrie eleison = Lord, have mercy. Christe eleison = Christ, have mercy.

Lord, You Are Holy (Sanctus)

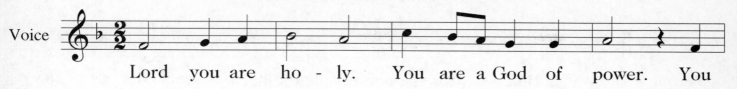

Lord you are ho - ly. You are a God of power. You

glo - ry is ev - ry - where. Ho - san - na!

ANYTIME SONGS (GATHERING, OFFERING, EUCHARIST)

Blessed Are the Pure in Heart for They Shall See God

Bles-sed are the pure in heart, for they shall see God;

bles-sed are the pure in heart for they shall see God.

Blessed Are You Now and Forever

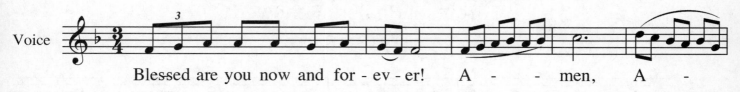

Blessed are you now and for - ev - er! A - - men, A -

men, A_____ men!

But as for Me and my Household

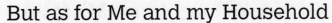

But as for me and my house-hold, we will serve the

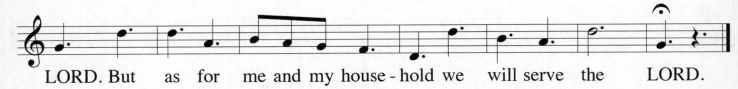

LORD. But as for me and my house-hold we will serve the LORD.

Draw Us to Your Center, O Lord

Draw us to your cen-ter, O Lord, help us fo-cus on your Word.

For, in your Word we live for-ev-er; draw us to your cen-ter, O Lord.

HAND MOTIONS FOR THE SONG: measures 1 - 4 slowly trace a circle, mm 5-6 make a rolling motion, mm 7-8 slowly trace a circle again.

Forgiven, Healed, Renewed

A Six - part round

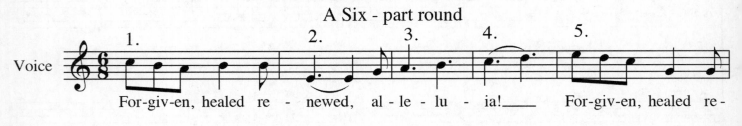

For-giv-en, healed re-newed, al-le-lu-ia!___ For-giv-en, healed re-

newed, al--le-lu--ia!_____

Gather Our Hearts, O God

Giver of Life, We Thank You

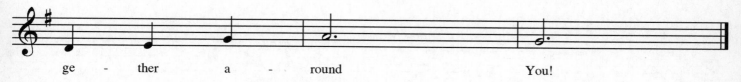

Giver of Life, We Thank You (Choral Version)

God Be Us!

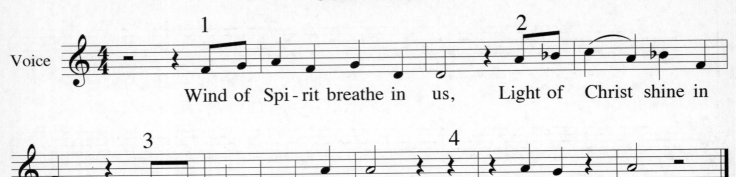

Wind of Spi-rit breathe in us, Light of Christ shine in us, Word of God be on our tongue, God be us!

Help Us, O Lord

A four-part round

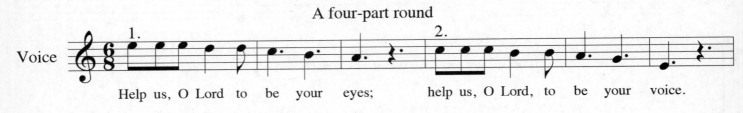

Help us, O Lord to be your eyes; help us, O Lord, to be your voice.

Help us, O Lord, to be your smile;— help us, O Lord to be your love in

all the world!

* in the song are for claps!

Hiney Ma Tov

CLAP on the accents below !!

Hi - ney ma tov u - ma na - yim   A - do - nai la - nu!

Hey!

Hi - ney ma tov u - ma na - yim   E - man - nu - el!

It's Time!

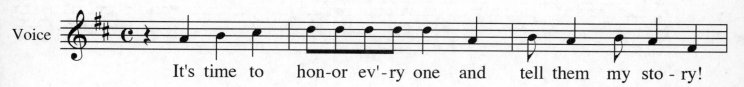

It's time to hon-or ev'-ry one and tell them my sto - ry!

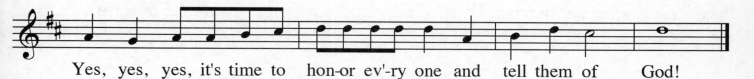

Yes, yes, yes, it's time to hon-or ev'-ry one and tell them of God!

Jesus, Help Me Love You More

Je - sus help me love you more; lov - ing, serv - ing, liv - ing, giv - ing.

Hold my hand, pass through faith's door; Lov - ing, serv - ing, liv - ing, giv - ing.

Jesus, You Are My Song

Je-sus, you are my song! Sing love, sing peace, to you my heart does be-long!

Sing calm, sing joy. Keep me with you for - ev - er!

Let Us Sing Our Song

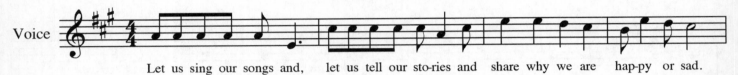

Let us sing our songs and, let us tell our sto-ries and share why we are hap-py or sad.

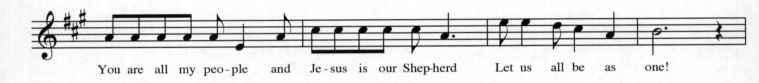

You are all my peo-ple and Je-sus is our Shep-herd Let us all be as one!

For the Spi-rit calls us to live as cho-sen peo-ple Praise the name of the Lord!

Lord, Give Us Times of Quiet Stillness

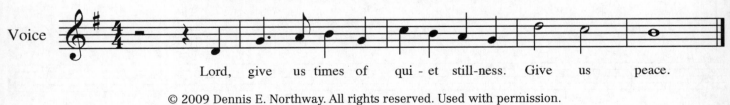

Lord, give us times of qui - et still-ness. Give us peace.

O Give Thanks to the Lord (F Major)

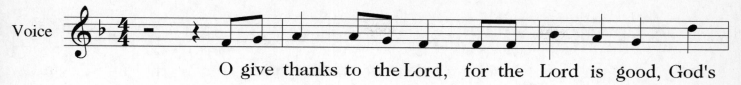

Voice

O give thanks to the Lord, for the Lord is good, God's

mer - cy en dures for - ev - er.

O Give Thanks to the Lord (Gb Major)

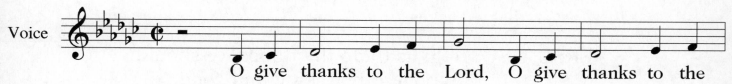

Voice

O give thanks to the Lord, O give thanks to the

Lord, for the Lord is good, God's mer - cy en - dures for - ev -

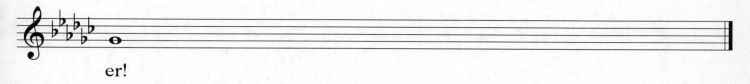

er!

O God, We Thank You for the Night

O God we thank you for the night, and

for the plea-sant mor-ning light; for rest and food and lov-ing care and

all that makes the day so fair!

VERSE TWO: Help us to do the things we should,
to be to others kind and good;
in all we do in work or play,
to grow more loving every day.

O How Awesome is This Place

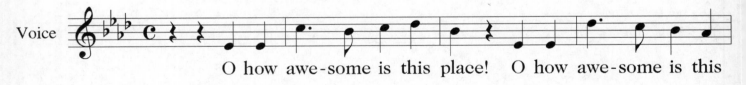

O how awe-some is this place! O how awe-some is this

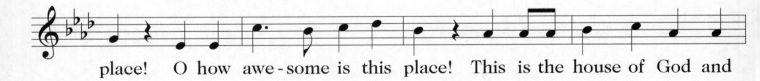

place! O how awe-some is this place! This is the house of God and

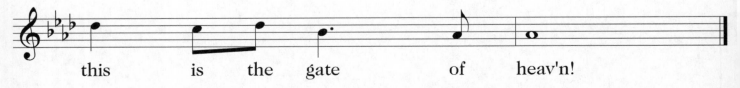

this is the gate of heav'n!

Peace, My Friends

Peace my friends I wish for you; God's peace be with us

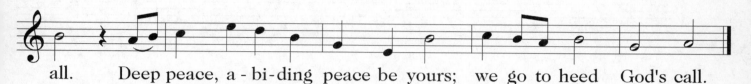

all. Deep peace, a-bi-ding peace be yours; we go to heed God's call.

Prepare Our Souls

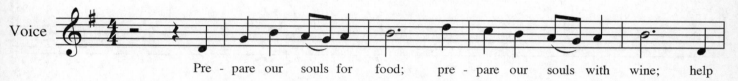

Pre-pare our souls for food; pre-pare our souls with wine; help

then us all to be-come good, and at Your ta-ble dine.

Seek and Serve

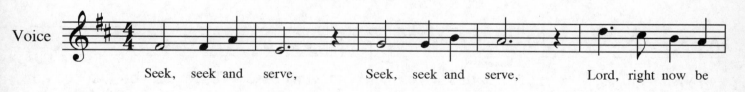

Seek, seek and serve, Seek, seek and serve, Lord, right now be

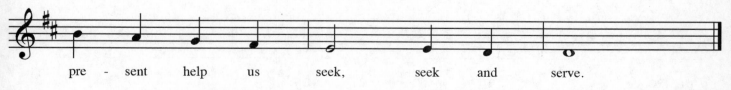

pre-sent help us seek, seek and serve.

Seek, Search and Renew

Sisters and Brothers I Wish You Peace

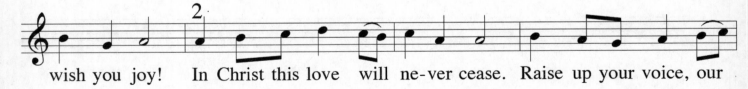

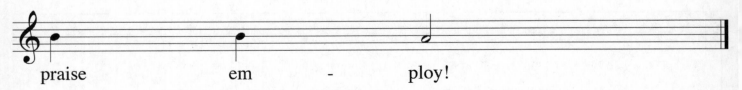

Story Dance!

This is the sto-ry of God's love for us;   this is the sto-ry of

our love for God! Our sto-ries dance! Our sto-ries dance! Let our sto-ries dance!

Those That Eat This Bread

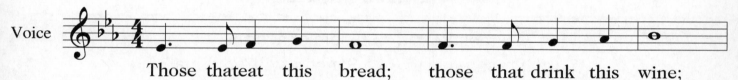

Those that eat this bread;   those that drink this wine;

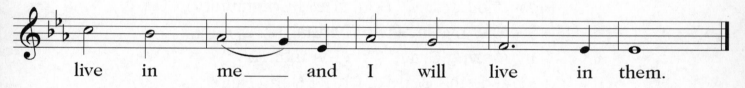

live   in   me____   and   I   will   live   in   them.

We Are All Children of God

We are all child-ren of God,   Ev-ry one of ev-ry   age.

Fa-ther, sis-ter, friend   Bro-ther, moth-er, stran-ger, all!   We are all child-ren of God!

We Are the Family Tree of God

OTHER SONGS WE HAVE FOUND AGE APPROPRIATE IN THE RITE PLACE:

Israeli Round / Shalom chaverim

Lord, Prepare Me to Be a Sanctuary (traditional)

Be Still and Know That I Am God (Iona Community)

Bless the Lord, My Soul (Taize Community)

Day by Day (The Hymnal 1982)

Amazing Grace (The Hymnal 1982)

This Is the Body of Christ (John Bell)

Section Four:

Resources

Starting Your Own Rite Place

So, you think you are interested in starting a worship service that is geared towards families with children. Where do you begin? We invite you to work and pray and spend time discerning some of these questions.

Where Are You Going? How Did You Get to This Place?

Why? Why do you find yourself in this position?

Who is your target audience?

How does the new idea fit into God's mission in your congregation?

What risks are you willing to take in spreading the gospel?

How open is your congregation open to making change?

How can you use your space?

Where is God in these thoughts?

How does it help to spread the gospel?

Will it make a difference?

Who Are You Taking With You?

What staffing is needed? Musicians? Clergy? Laity? Christian formation leaders? Liturgists? Administrative staff?

Do you want a committee to discuss the idea and do the planning?

How does it impact the work of the Altar Guild?

Do you have the personnel to make it succeed? (People with the gifts and knowledge of worship and child development?)

How Will You Get There? What Do You Need in Place?

What budget do you need?

Who will make the liturgical decisions?

What music do you want to use?

Will you use a prayer book Liturgy or prepare your own?

What day and time?

What formation do you need to prepare the congregation?

Do you want to adjust a current service or start a new one? Experience tells us that this kind of service is best done as a new adventure.

Are you prepared to welcome in your guests and new members?

How will you use your space? What space will you use? Church? Parish Hall?

What will participants see and hear and how will they interpret it?

Other Questions:

What music will you use?

Do you want to have Holy Communion?

What symbols do you want to use?

How will you advertise?

How does that impact other worship services?

Are you prepared for this liturgy to change you (or your church)?

Are you prepared for the energy that it can bring and take?

Are you ready for the movement of the Holy Spirit?

Do you have the energy to start something new?

Will it be child-centered or child-friendly?

What is God's mission for your congregation?

Preparing the Space

Whenever you plan a new liturgy, it is always critical to bring on board those who will be getting everything ready for the service. The Altar Guild is typically the group who prepares the space and many of the items needed for the service at Grace, where we offer two services on a Sunday, the first one being *The Rite Place* at 9:00 a.m.

On Saturday, Altar Guild members prepare two supply baskets, which they leave in the working Sacristy for the Presider, deacon, or any other adult to assemble on early Sunday morning.

Supplies

Basket No. 1

- One finger bowl (lavabo)
- Four wooden patens (or bowls for bread)
- Processional paten (for bread to be placed in for procession)
- Four glass chalices (small wine glasses)
- Four purificator towels (for wiping the chalices at communion)
- One finger towel (lavabo linen)
- One larger towel (corporal) used by deacon
- One small non-liturgical towel or cloth (for use by a child or adult with hand sanitizer)
- Two candles on the altar (battery operated is best so that children will not get burned as they gather around the table/altar)
- Altar frontal
- Bread, wine and water
- Hand sanitizer (such as Purell®) in a dispenser
- If Sunday is a non-white vestment day, put a couple napkins in that match the liturgical color of the vestments.
- Small brass bell, cushion, and wooden striker (a singing bowl also works)
- Gluten-free wafer/bread in a Pyx or small container

Basket No. 2

- Four large aprons for the communion ministers (wine)
- Four small aprons for the Communion ministers (bread)
- Storytelling log (rain stick)
- Wooden cross or other crosses

A note on aprons: Different colors, to coordinate with the liturgical calendar, can be used accordingly:

Season or Occasion	Color	Sizes Available
Advent	Blue	Adult and Child
Baptisms Christmas Easter	White	Adult and Child
Epiphany Liturgical "ordinary" time (Season of Pentecost)	Green	Adult and Child
Lent	Off white	Adult and Child *These aprons have word "Lent" marked on them*
Pentecost Sunday Specific Feast Days	Red	Adult and Child

Set-Up

1. Altar
   a. Candles hold frontal piece.
      i. Place so the frontal piece shows cross pattern.
      ii. Confirm it hangs evenly
      iii. Place basket with towels and wooden patens close by the side of altar.
   b. Deacon's job is to "set the Table"—so leave patens, lavabo bowel and towels in the basket.
   c. It IS okay to put the hand sanitizer on the altar.
2. Storyteller's chair
3. Use square back chair—it makes it easy to hang aprons from either side.
   a. Leave rain stick (log) on floor, by East (right side if you are facing the chair) side of the storyteller's chair (children like regular patterns and this helps them to be more self-sufficient).
   b. Take singing bell, cushion and ringer out of their box.
      i. Put them on the small table on West side (left side if you are facing the chair) of the storyteller's chair.
      ii. Bell rests on the cushion, on top of the box.

      iii. Hang aprons on back of storyteller's chair.

      iv. Children's small aprons (sign of servant ministry) on West side (used for bread givers).

      v. Large adult-size aprons on the East side (used for chalice bearers).

4. Baskets

   a. Place offering baskets on either side of main aisle in front of first row or pews.

   b. Confirm with the musician or presider whether processional items will be used (small crosses, bells, musical instruments, etc.); if they will, place a third, larger basket in the center aisle at the front before the altar area for the congregation to deposit the items in when they arrive in front—this way there will be no fighting over the items during the service.

Sunday Morning Preparation Activities

1. Turn on lights.

2. Unlock vesting sacristy if it is locked. Place offering pouches out for each service.

3. Unlock doors to the sanctuary.

4. Place worship programs at all entrances to the sanctuary.

5. Place 4 copies of the day's bulletin in the Vesting Sacristy.

6. Prepare entrance of the Church by the Baptismal Font (This can also be done on Sunday morning.)

   a. Confirm small table is in middle of aisle and has a small linen on it.

   b. On the table, place:

      i. Wooden Cross

      ii. Wine and water cruets

      iii. Communion bread on processional paten (plate or basket)

7. Candles may be lit 10–15 minutes before service begins.

   a. Light Paschal candle (Baptism and Easter season only).

   b. Light primary votive candle at both sides:

      i. West side—St. Mary side altar

      ii. East side—Icon area

   c. Turn on battery operated altar candles.

8. Confirm seating arrangement is appropriate.

Prepared by Alfred Papillon, Altar Guild Coordinator
Grace Episcopal Church, Oak Park, Illinois

Post-Service Activities

Volunteer worshipers normally move the children's altar (table) out of the crossing.

The Altar area

1. Secure the offertory collection.
    a. Place in safe spot in Working Sacristy.
    b. Note date, time, and number of participants in the service (attendance).
2. Gather accouterments of worship.
3. Put in the first basket:
    a. Chalices, patens
    b. Altar Linens
    c. Return singing bell & ringer to their box.
4. Put in second basket:
    a. Aprons
    b. Story-telling log (rain stick)
    c. Wooden cross

The Consecrated (Blessed) Elements

Have someone dispose of the unconsumed Elements (consecrated wine and bread) at this point. The Rector has provided the following options:

1. Unconsumed wine is poured into the piscina (sink that sends contents directly to the earth) and bread returned to the earth (see point 3).
2. If there is a minimal amount of bread and wine, members of the clergy, Altar Guild, or faith community personally consume the remaining elements.
3. It is allowed to pour wine and bread into the ground. In our parish, locations that have been used are:
    a. On the West side under the bush that is immediately outside the door on the left you; may place the bread broken into small pieces on the ground.
    b. Under the great tree in the NE corner of the back yard of the Rectory.

Worship Space

1. Sweep up crumbs from altar, floor by altar and communion stations.
2. Afterwards:
    a. Sweep floor by votive areas.
    b. Scrape up any large wax spill, if noticed.
    c. Extinguish candles, if tall enough, replace with others for next worship service.

3. Candles

    a. Pillar candles

        i. Don't extinguish pillar candles immediately.

        ii. Leave them burning until ready to crop, so the wax cuts more readily.

        iii. Take pillar candles into working sacristy and cut them down. A suitable knife is in sink cabinet, in the right hand drawer.

        iv. Votive candles,

    b. Extinguish; if long enough, put them out for reuse.

    c. Sift through sand to take out any wax clumps, debris.

    d. Either smooth out the sand or draw an inviting pattern.

Prepared by Alfred Papillon, Altar Guild Coordinator
Grace Episcopal Church, Oak Park, Illinois

Preparing the Readings

Let the little children come to me, and do not stop them; for it is to such as these that the kingdom of heaven belongs.   (Matthew 19:14)

Our principles in preparing the lesson/s to be read during The Rite Place include accessibility as well as accuracy. Episcopalians are "People of the Book." We believe the Holy Scriptures of the Old and New Testaments to be the Word of God, and to contain all things necessary to salvation (*BCP*, p. 538). We believe that all hearers—young or old, disabled or gifted—are able to learn from the Bible *as it is* written. Even though many may hear the readings differently, scripture usually works on multiple levels. We try to use vocabulary written in a style accessible to a young child throughout our liturgy, but children's Bibles unnecessarily simplify stories, making them unsuitable for adult listeners.

Since this liturgy is aimed at young *and* old, we wish to make it accessible to the young (without insulting intelligence of elders), adults who were not raised in the church, and both groups who don't necessarily know the meaning of churchy language and jargon.

Most English translations can only be used with care. Scholarly translations (*New Revised Standard Version* or *New English Bible*) are very accurate, but use traditional jargon and lose the everyday sense of the original. For example: baptism vs. washing, heaven vs. sky. Popular translations that have more accessible language include the *Good News Bible* and *The Message*, however they are often paraphrased, allowing cultural biases of the translator to come through. These also often use traditional jargon.

The deacon at Grace prepares the Bible readings each week, seeking an accessible vocabulary and style. In advance, he reviews the text using *NRSV* and Lattimore and compares popular translations—*Good News Bible*, *The Message*, and *Easy-to-Read Version* (World Bible Translation Center)—that are available with the exception of *Lattimore* at www.biblegateway.com. He reviews them all to substitute easier synonyms for words/phrases beyond the early elementary oral vocabulary level.

Prepared by Jonathan Baumgarten, Deacon
Grace Episcopal Church, Oak Park, Illinois

Preparing a Homily

Every week, we take the time to break open the texts of the Bible, of the assembly, and of the world when we share our thoughts in the homily. It is best to limit this talk to five minutes or less. Speaking for much longer than that will stretch the attention span of most young children, and of many adults. I have found that it is difficult to judge time while I am speaking, so I find these rules of thumb help me stick to the time limit:

- If I am speaking from notes or some form of outline, it should fit on one index card, or

- If I have written out a full script, it should fill about ½ page when using usual printer fonts and margins.

It is best to speak as extemporaneously as possible. When you write out a sermon or speech, there is a strong tendency to make those remarks grammatically correct, and to fail to capture the rhythms of spoken speech. Remember, the rules found in *The Elements of Style* are those of written English. Spoken English is substantially different. That isn't too much of a problem when you are preaching from a pulpit to a congregation seated quietly in rows, but that level of formality feels pretentious in an intimate setting like The Rite Place. And, that pretentiousness can form an obstacle to the listeners being able to understand what you are trying to convey.

An additional advantage to speaking extemporaneously is that you can watch your listeners for their reactions. If your listeners seem confused by something you say, you can give them more explanation, or explain it differently. Or, if you seem to be losing their attention, you can try a different tack, or you can wrap-up more quickly. In any case, you aren't restricted by the text you have written out.

When I begin to prepare a Rite Place homily, I'm often filled with anxiety over the blank page in front of me. I'm purportedly an adult, I don't teach children for a living, and I spend most of my days talking to and writing for adults. I don't know where to start. In general, my sermon preparations fall into two broad categories:

- Since I am usually already preparing a sermon for the same day for adult listeners, I can start with that. A short version of the adult sermon often works well. (By the way, if you can't summarize your sermon for an older audience in one paragraph, you need to work more on tightening-up your adult sermon.) You often can just select one concept from the larger sermon, and explain it more simply—with a limited vocabulary and shorter sentences.

- Be open to the working of the Spirit. Sometimes during preparation a different topic will present itself. One that will be more easily understood by children or that will be easier to illustrate. If you have a thought like that, don't be afraid of it. Since you are trying to be extemporaneous in your preaching, you can be more flexible with changing what you will say, or how you say it. On rare occasions, the children's sermon has captured my imagination and I ended up expanding it for the adult sermon.

I find that it is good to begin a Rite Place homily with either dialog or illustrative story. An illustrative story should generally involve childhood or children, and will introduce or amplify the point you are trying to make. It can be taken from your own youth or family, or from children that you have known. Stories from your experience have the advantage of having a core of truth, and your delivery will be usually be much more engaging. You should avoid canned stories—in an intimate setting like The Rite Place they often ring false.

A Rite Place homily can also begin with a dialog with the congregation, especially the children. This need not be complicated, just ask the children what they know or think about the subject of your sermon. The crucial thing here is to not over simplify the topic, but to speak carefully — using vocabulary appropriate to young children, and using simple sentences. If you pay attention to what the children are saying, you can generally transition into the rest of your sermon. But be sure to listen respectfully to the children, and make eye contact. If you want them to care about what you have to say, you have to care about what they have to say.

Now, based on mishaps that I have witnessed, there are a few things to avoid. Avoid speaking for too long. Your listener's attention span is limited. If your thoughts are truly organized, you don't need that much time to explain them.

Avoid jargon. Let me repeat that—avoid jargon. Let me repeat that again—avoid jargon. Jargon is the great evil at The Rite Place. When you are preaching, use Anglo-Saxon words (if you're preaching in English) when you can. For almost any concept, there are synonyms in English. Use the Anglo-Saxon option as much as you are able, since it will briefer, punchier, and more likely to be part of a young child's vocabulary. If you find yourself in a spot where polysyllabic or Latinate words are absolutely necessary (and they usually are not), then define them with one and two-syllable words. And, if you end up being tempted to use any of these words, be very, very careful, or just find a new topic:

- hermeneutic

- midrash

- Parousia

- Eschaton

- Apologetics

- (I could go on, but you get the idea.)

Another danger is losing control of the room. Be sure to keep the children on the subject during a dialog. Children will often go off on a tangent. They will make connections that have been educated out of us adults. Sometimes those connections will be excellent, and sometimes they will be wrong, but they are just acting their age. When they go off on a tangent, don't panic or mock them. It is often best to acknowledge what they have offered, and then gently return to your point.

A final thing to avoid for your homilies is reading a children's book or story. The Rite Place is not the right venue. There is usually not enough explanation in a story, and the point of a homily is to offer an explanation of some part of a story we heard earlier in the liturgy from the Bible. Also, although The Rite Place is an intimate venue, to appreciate an illustrated children's book requires being even closer than is possible in a liturgical setting. Finally, except for books aimed at babies, children's books are usually too long. You really want to limit The Rite Place homily to five minutes.

Above all, have fun. Be prepared to be moved by the "aha" moments that the children have. Open your own mind to the insights that they offer to the text that you broke open for them. Or did they really open it for you?

Prepared by Jonathan Baumgarten, Deacon
Grace Episcopal Church, Oak Park, Illinois

A Presider's Customary for The Rite Place

Grace Episcopal Church, Oak Park
9:00 a.m. Service (thirty minute service)

Beginning of Each Season

- Make a new bulletin in the leader's binder (black and white picture of Jesus as Good Shepherd on the cover).
- Underline all of the leader's lines.
- Select the objects that will be brought in.

Vestments for This Service

- September to early June: albs and a stole (there is a stole with children on it)
- Summer: shorts, slacks, shirt, collar or no collar, and stole

Preparation—Sunday Morning Before the Service *(by presider or deacon and sometimes Musician)*

- Take the binder to the entrance of the church.
- Assign a leader (ask someone as they are entering the church).
- Verify that the Altar Guild has placed all items in their appropriate places (They have a binder in the working sacristy with all the information that is needed).
- We read one lesson. Add the gospel reading or the lesson chosen by the preacher to the gospel book and it put on the table near the baptismal font. Jon, our deacon usually does this.
- Add batteries to the wireless microphone (found in the left drawer of the desk in the sacristy). Make sure that the presider, deacon, and preacher all have microphones.
- Be back by the baptismal font shortly before 9:55 to help greet people and begin the singing.
- If there is a supply priest or musician, review the service with them.
- If you are the supply priest or musician, check with the deacon or assigned person from Grace to review the service.

Singing and Beginning of Service

- Hand out bulletins and greet people.
- Assist the musician with singing the songs.
- Assign the worship leader (just ask and you will usually get a volunteer).
- Dennis, the musician, will ask if it is time to start and you get to reply, "Yes."
- If needed, assist the worship leader with the opening sentence.

Procession

- Join the procession near the end and make sure that all the items (cross, cruets, and gospel book) have been picked up by a volunteer.
- Process down to the Crossing.
- Sit in any empty seat or on the floor.

Liturgy of the Word

- With the deacon make sure that the Worship Leader is ready to start the collect.
- People will sit in the chairs and in the pews.
- Musician gives the rain stick to someone to use during the gospel.
- Deacon (presider when the deacon is missing) will read the gospel from the storyteller chair.
- Musician will lead all of the music.
- Sermon can be done from the chair or standing or moving around. Sermon is not much longer than five minutes.
- Preacher rings the bell (singing bowl) at the end of the sermon. It is typically on a small table next to the storyteller chair.

Peace, Announcements and Offertory

- Announce the Peace.
- Greet people for a few minutes.
- Presider or Deacon: Ask if there is anyone who would like to help give out the bread and the wine. Also ask if there is anyone who has not done it for a while who would like to volunteer. Pass out the aprons to the volunteers–4 short aprons for bread. 4 long aprons for wine. Aprons are attached to the storyteller chair. We chose aprons because they give a sense of servant ministry.
- Remind someone to get the Offertory baskets to collect the gift of money. They are located next to the first pews.
- Welcome folks to Grace and introduce yourself.
- Make announcements and see what people have other announcements.
- Take a moment to explain that all are welcome to receive communion and that the kids will be giving out the bread and the wine.
- While you are making announcements and all the other tasks, the deacon will begin to the set the table with those giving out communion. The Deacon will wash the hands of the kids and then wash the Presider's hands. If there is not a Deacon, ask for a volunteer to help set the table with the kids.

Liturgy of the Table

- Presider sits in the storyteller chair for the Eucharistic prayer. Congregation is seated.

- After the song, ring the bell (singing bowl). Let the silence stay until it feels uncomfortable. All will enjoy this time.

- The kids will raise the bread and wine. The Deacon will assist with this part.

- Cross yourself for, "Send the Holy Spirit upon us…"

- All will put their hands out towards the bread and the wine for the calling of the Holy Spirit.

- Stand up for the "Great Amen."

- Take a deep breath after the very rowdy Amen and begin the Lord's Prayer. Have hands cupped upwards in front of you. This helps to center the kids.

- Break the bread.

- Assist the deacon or other adult helper with giving the bowls for the bread and the bread to the bread givers. Assist (when they will let you) with the breaking of the bread. Assist the deacon with handing out the chalices of wine. It is helpful to have the kids stand up before giving them the chalices.

- Be attentive to someone who is new at this ministry so you can tell them what to say.

- Help get the kids and adults settled behind and to the side of the storyteller chair for the distribution of the Communion.

- Two breads and two wines on each side.

- Stand in front of the storyteller chair with the gluten-free wafers.

- Invite the congregation to come forward to receive Communion.

- Many people will go to light candles in the two side chapel areas.

- With the deacon, watch to see when Communion is almost over.

- Look to see if there is anyone who cannot come forward to receive Communion.

- Assist the Communion ministers with giving Communion to one another and taking the bowls and chalices to the Credence Table. It is behind and to the right of the storyteller chair.

- Make sure the Leader has his/her binder and is ready to start the post Communion prayer. This is sometimes done when people are still lighting candles.

- Pronounce the blessing.

- Announce whether or not there is Sunday School/Catechesis of the Good Shepherd (Montessori Christian Formation) and invite them to gather at the arches to join the Catechist and other children.

- Remind them about coffee hour.

- Invite the assembly to help get the space ready for the next service.

Prepared by Shawn Schreiner, Rector
Grace Episcopal Church, Oak Park, Illinois

Top Ten Reasons for Building a Solid Leadership Team

Caveats:

- Your mileage may vary.
- Directions to a destination are only helpful if you know where you want to go.
- Please accept these as offerings—not absolute statements of truth.

1. If liturgy is the "work of the people," then Job One is gathering the people who can commit to doing the Work. Ritual is the public enactment of commonly held values, it takes a while to commonly hold certain values.

   The invitation you offer the world needs a core team already modeling the practices that build the community you hope to lead.

2. No church exists in a vacuum; only clubs do and all too quickly.

   Move out into your neighboring culture as quickly as you can. Developing a vision for ministry is neither a solo activity, nor is it the whole community's work. It is a leadership team's work.

   Our public gatherings are validated by the presence of the Stranger in our midst.

3. Worship is "gather-teach-bless-break"—get to gathering or you might break before you're blessed.

   Since most of those who will eventually join have no prior experience with being in community, they will need committed mentors for at least the first 18 months. Otherwise, you are doing that mentoring on your own.

4. Good worship is prayed over before enjoyed, like any shared meal among God's children. Take your time setting the Table.

   You need a group of people to do discernment and imagine in partnership with you. (Deep listening in context and evangelism—you need partners for that early piece.)

5. If you make it all about you, all you will attract is rams and ewes.

   Your tendency will be to stay a family-sized church with one or two good hosts and a good sturdy coffee table ministry.

   Pastoral care is best when offered by the community. That takes a cadre of leaders trained to offer those ministry practices. Without it, your are still offering heroic leadership—not a good start for a new community.

   Timelines go backward and forward in time, make one with your core team and celebrate the stops along your line from inception toward God's deeper purpose for your community.

You need to gel before you can effectively evan-gel-ize. Work together to share the Gospel.

Difference between the practices of calling a core team and the practices of gathering a congregation.

Developing a timeline for gathering a core team that focuses on the development of leadership and the luxury of discerning other's expectations and strengths.

Jesus sent out pairs for conversation, not clever masters of ceremonies.

You never get a second chance at a first expression. What is the uniqueness of your faith community that you want the guest to "come and see"?

Worship is worthship, showing God how worthy God is of praise. It is not a marketing tool. We build communities of faith invitation by invitation, not by marketing.

Developed by Stephanie Spellers, James Hamilton, and Tom Brackett from the "1st Friday at 4 Ministry Innovators Round Table Gathering," May 2, 2014. Used with permission.

Christian Formation Songs

Advent / Christmas / Epiphany

Jesus, You are Light

Light Up my Heart!

Light to Scatter the Darkness

Prepare Me, O Lord

Tell the Watchmen the King is Coming!

Lent

Ash Wednesday Song

We Are in Lent

Palm Sunday

Prepare the Way for the King!

Maundy Thursday

We're Gathered in an Ash-filled Lent

Good Friday

Blessed Be, O Christ

Glory Be to Jesus–refrain and three stanzas

We Adore You O Christ, and We Bless You

Eastertide

Easter Flowers

Ev'ry Day, Just Like On Easter

Halleluia, Christ is Risen Again!

Pentecost

Stir Up the Flame

Baptism

There is One Body and One Spirit

We Thank You God for the Gift of Water

Rogation & Pet Blessing

Bless the Birds and Beasties Too!

These Are All a Gift from God

Liturgy Songs (Amens, Sanctus, Prayer Responses)

Amen 1

Amen 2

Amen 3

Glory to You, O Christ (Gospel Acclamation)

God, We Have Made You Glad. Bless Us. (Prayers of the People response)

God, We Have Made You Sad. Bless Us. (Prayers of the People response)

Hear Our Prayer (Prayers of the People response)

Hear Us, Good Lord (Prayers of the People response)

Hear Us Lord of Light (Prayers of the People response)

Jubliate Deo

Kyrie

Lord, You are Holy (Sanctus)

Anytime Songs (Gathering, Offering, Eucharist)

Blessed are the pure in heart for they shall see God

Blessed Are You Now and Forever

But as for Me and My Household

Draw Us to Your Center, O Lord

Forgiven, Healed, Renewed

Gather Our Hearts, O God

Giver of Life, We Thank You

Giver of Life, We Thank You (Choral Version)

God be Us!

Help Us, O Lord

Hiney Ma Tov

It's Time!

Jesus, Help Me Love You More

Jesus, You Are My Song

Let Us Sing Our Songs

Lord, Give Us Times of Quiet Stillness

O Give Thanks to the Lord (F Major)

O Give Thanks to the Lord (Gb Major)

O God, We Thank You for the Night

O How Awesome is This Place

Peace, My Friends

Prepare Our Souls

Seek and Serve

Seek, Search and Renew

Sisters and Brothers I Wish You Peace

Story Dance!

Those That Eat This Bread

We Are All Children of God

We Are the Family Tree of God

CHILDREN'S CHARTER

THE EPISCOPAL CHURCH

FOR THE CHURCH

Nurture of

Children are a heritage from the LORD, and the fruit of the womb is a gift. — Psalm 127:4 (BCP)

THE CHURCH IS CALLED:

♦ to receive, nurture and treasure each child as a gift from God;

♦ to proclaim the Gospel to children, in ways that empower them to receive and respond to God's love;

♦ to give high priority to the quality of planning for children and the preparation and support of those who minister with them;

♦ to include children, in fulfillment of the Baptismal Covenant, as members and full participants in the Eucharistic community and in the church's common life of prayer, witness and service.

Ministry to THE CHILD

Then Jesus took the children in his arms, placed his hands on each of them and blessed them.— Mark 10:16

THE CHURCH IS CALLED:

♦ to love, shelter, protect and defend children within its own community and in the world, especially those who are abused, neglected or in danger;

♦ to nurture and support families in caring for their children, acting in their children's best interest, and recognizing and fostering their children's spirituality and unique gifts;

♦ to embrace children who seek Christian nurture independently of their parents' participation in the church;

♦ to advocate for the integrity of childhood and the dignity of all children at every level of our religious, civic and political structures.

Ministry of THE CHILD

A child shall lead them — Isaiah 11:6

THE CHURCH IS CALLED:

♦ to receive children's special gifts as signs of the Reign of God;

♦ to foster community beyond the family unit, in which children, youth and adults know each other by name, minister to each other, and are partners together in serving Christ in the world;

♦ to appreciate children's abilities and readiness to represent Christ and his church, to bear witness to him wherever they may be, and according to gifts given them, to carry on Christ's work of reconciliation in the world, and to take their place in the life, worship, and governance of the church. *(Ministry of the Laity pg. 855 BCP)*

For more information: www.episcopalchurch.org/myp   1-800-334-7626 ext 5212
Developed by the Episcopal Dioceses of Alaska, Bethlehem, Central New York, Chicago, Dallas, Hawaii, Iowa, Massachusetts, Mexico, Southwest Florida, Western North Carolina, Wyoming, and The Office of Children's Ministries for the Episcopal Church   56-9601-2

The Charter For
Lifelong Christian Formation

*Lifelong Christian Faith Formation in The Episcopal Church is
Lifelong growth in the knowledge, service and love of God as followers of
Christ and is informed by Scripture, Tradition and Reason.*

I have called you friends. John 15:14-16

Through The Episcopal Church, God Invites all people:

· To enter into a prayerful life of worship, continuous learning, intentional outreach, advocacy and service.

· To hear the Word of God through scripture, to honor church teachings, and continually to embrace the joy of Baptism and Eucharist, spreading the Good News of the risen Christ and ministering to all.

· To respond to the needs of our constantly changing communities, as Jesus calls us, in ways that reflect our diversity and cultures as we seek, wonder and discover together.

· To hear what the Spirit is saying to God's people, placing ourselves in the stories of our faith, thereby empowering us to proclaim the Gospel message.

*You did not choose me,
but I chose you and appointed you to go and bear fruit. John 15:14-16*

Through The Episcopal Church, God Inspires all people:

· To experience Anglican liturgy, which draws us closer to God, helps us discern God's will and encourages us to share our faith journeys.

· To study Scripture, mindful of the context of our societies and cultures, calling us to seek truth anew while remaining fully present in the community of faith.

· To develop new learning experiences, equipping disciples for life in a world of secular challenges and carefully listening for the words of modern sages who embody the teachings of Christ.

· To prepare for a sustainable future by calling the community to become guardians of God's creation.

I am giving you these commands that you may love one another. John 15:17

Through The Episcopal Church, God Transforms all people:

· By doing the work Jesus Christ calls us to do, living into the reality that we are all created in the image of God and carrying out God's work of reconciliation, love, forgiveness, healing, justice and peace.

· By striving to be a loving and witnessing community, which faithfully confronts the tensions in the church and the world as we struggle to live God's will.

· By seeking out diverse and expansive ways to empower prophetic action, evangelism, advocacy and collaboration in our contemporary global context.

· By holding all accountable to lift every voice in order to reconcile oppressed and oppressor to the love of God in Jesus Christ our Lord.

*Christian Faith Formation in The Episcopal Church is a lifelong journey
with Christ, in Christ, and to Christ.*

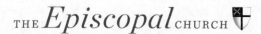

For more information: www.episcopalchurch.org 1-800-334-7626 ext. 6051
Approved by General Convention 2009 - Resolution A082

El Estatuto para la
Formación Crisiana Continua

La Formación en la Fe Cristiana Continua en la Iglesia Episcopal es crecimiento continuo
en el conocimiento, el servicio y el amor de Dios como seguidores de Cristo
y es transmitida por las Escrituras, la Tradición y la Razón.

Los he llamado amigos. Juan 15:14-16

A Través de La Iglesia Episcopal, Dios Inivita a todas las personas a:

•Entrar en una vida piadosa de adoración, aprendizaje continuo, servicio social intencionado, el apoyo activo y el servicio.

•Escuchar la Palabra de Dios a través de las Escrituras, para honrar las enseñanzas de la iglesia, y abrazar continuamente la alegría del Bautismo y la Eucaristía, divulgando la Buena Nueva del Cristo resucitado y ministrando para todos.

•Responder a las necesidades de nuestras comunidades constantemente cambiantes, como nos lo demanda Jesús, en maneras que reflejen nuestra diversidad y culturas mientras buscamos, nos hacemos preguntas y descubrimos juntos.

•Escuchar lo que el Espíritu le esta diciendo al pueblo de Dios, ubicándonos a nosotros mismos en las historias de nuestra fe, y de ese modo, inspirándonos para proclamar el mensaje del Evangelio.

No me escogieron ustedes a mi,
sino que yo los escogí a ustedes y los comisioné para que vayan y den fruto. Juan15:14-16

A Través de La Iglesia Episcopal, Dios Inspira a todas las personas a:

•Experimentar la liturgia Anglicana, la cual nos acerca a Dios, nos ayuda a discernir la voluntad de Dios y nos alienta a compartir nuestras jornadas de fe.

•Estudiar las Escrituras, conscientes del contexto de nuestras sociedades y culturas, demandándonos de nuevo la búsqueda de la verdad, mientras nos mantenemos completamente presentes en la comunidad de fe.

•Desarrollar nuevas experiencias de aprendizaje, equipando discípulos para la vida en un mundo de desafíos seculares y a escuchar atentamente las palabras de los sabios modernos quienes expresan las enseñanzas de Cristo.

•Prepararse para un futuro sostenible exhortando a la comunidad a transformarse en guardiana de la creación de Dios.

éste es mi mandamiento, que se amen los unos a los otros. Juan15:17

A través de La Iglesia Episcopal, Dios Transforma a todas las personas:

•Haciendo el trabajo que Jesús no ha llamado a hacer, viviendo en la realidad de que todos nosotros fuimos creados a la imagen de Dios y realizando el trabajo de Dios de reconciliación, amor, perdón, sanación, justicia y paz.

•Esforzándonos en ser una comunidad amorosa y testigo, la cual fielmente confronte las tensiones en la iglesia y el mundo mientras luchamos para vivir la voluntad de Dios.

•Buscando maneras expansivas y diversas para empoderar la acción profética, la evangelización, la ayuda activa y la colaboración en nuestro contexto contemporáneo global.

•Responsabilizándonos para impulsar todas las voces a fin de reconciliar al opresor y al oprimido por el amor de Dios en Jesucristo nuestro Señor.

La Formación de la fe Cristiana en La Iglesia Episcopal es una jornada continua de toda la vida,
con Cristo, en Cristo y para Cristo.

Por más información visite www.episcopalchurch.org o llame al 1-800-334-7626 extensión 6051.
La resolución AO82 aprobada por la Convención General de 2009